Printed at the Mathematical Centre, Kruislaan 413, Amsterdam, The Netherlands.

The Mathematical Centre, founded 11 February 1946, is a non-profit institution for the promotion of pure and applied mathematics and computer science. It is sponsored by the Netherlands Government through the Netherlands Organization for the Advancement of Pure Research (Z.W.O.).

MATHEMATICAL CENTRE TRACTS 163

MULTIPLE GRID METHODS FOR EQUATIONS OF THE SECOND KIND WITH APPLICATIONS IN FLUID MECHANICS

H. SCHIPPERS

MATHEMATISCH CENTRUM AMSTERDAM 1983

1980 Mathematics subject classification: 31A25, 65B99, 65F10, 65N20, 76B05, 76U05

ISBN 90 6196 260 9

Math Sep

TABLE OF CONTENTS

ACKNOWLEDGEMENTS

The author wishes to express his gratitude to the governing board of the "Stichting Mathematisch Centrum" for publishing this monograph that is based on his Doctor's Thesis prepared under the guidance of Prof. P. Wesseling of Delft University of Technology; his constructive criticism and remarks are greatly appreciated.

H. Schippers

CHAPTER 1

INTRODUCTION

In this thesis multiple grid methods are studied for solving the algebraic systems that occur in numerical methods for Fredholm equations of the second kind:

$$(1.1) \qquad f = Kf + g.$$

Let g belong to a Banach space X. We assume that the operator K is compact from X into X, and that (1.1) has a unique solution $f \in X$. For the description of the multiple grid techniques we use projection methods. Equations of the type (1.1) often arise in applications: potential problems, solid mechanics, diffraction problems, scattering in quantum mechanics, water waves, etc. (cf. [6], [7], [10], [11]). In the following sections we briefly review the concepts of compactness, projection methods and multiple grid methods.

1.1. COMPACT OPERATORS

Heuristically speaking, compact operators are operators that in general possess some kind of "smoothing property". The following definition is borrowed from ATKINSON [3]:

DEFINITION 1.1.1. Let X and Y be Banach spaces. A linear operator $K: X \to Y$ is called *compact* if for every bounded sequence $\{f_n\}$ in X, there is a subsequence $\{f_{n_j}\}$ such that $\{Kf_{n_j}\}$ converges in Y.
Equivalently, K maps bounded subsets of X into subsets with compact closure in Y.

A simple example of a compact operator is given by the following integral operator on $X = Y = C[0,1]$:

$$(1.2) \qquad Kf(x) = \int_0^1 k(x,y)f(y)dy,$$

where

$$\sup_{0 \le x \le 1} \int_0^1 |k(x,y)|dy < \infty$$

and

$$\lim_{\delta \to 0} \sup_{0 \le x \le 1} \int_0^1 |k(x+\delta,y) - k(x,y)|dy = 0.$$

By the Arzela-Ascoli theorem it follows that K is compact on C[0,1] (cf. [3]).

A more abstract example is given by Schauder inversion. Let Au = g (g belongs to a Banach space Y) be a quasilinear elliptic operator equation with:

$$Au = \Delta u + \vec{a}(u) \cdot \nabla u + b(u).$$

Define the linear operator

$$A_v u \equiv \Delta u + \vec{a}(v) \cdot \nabla v + b(v) \qquad \text{for fixed } v \in Z,$$

where the Banach space Z is a subspace of the Banach space X with Z compactly imbedded in X. If $A_v u = g$ has one and only one solution u = Kv satisfying the a priori estimate

$$\|u\|_Z \le C(R)\|g\|_Y, \qquad \forall g \in Y,$$

if $\|v\|_X < R$, then the non-linear operator K: X → X is compact (cf. [4]). The fixed points of

$$(1.3) \qquad u = Ku$$

coincide with the solutions of Au = g. In this thesis examples will be studied that are similar to (1.2) and (1.3).

1.2. PROJECTION METHODS

A description of our multiple grid techniques can be given by interpolatory projection operators. For the approximate solution of linear or nonlinear equations of the type (1.1) or (1.3) projection methods are well-known.

Let $\{X_N\}$ be a sequence of finite-dimensional subspaces of X with dimension N and assume that for every N we have a linear projection operator T_N which projects X into X_N. The projection method for solving (1.1) is: solve the approximate equation

$$(1.4) \qquad f_N = T_N K f_N + T_N g, \quad f_N \in X_N.$$

One can solve (1.4) by reducing it to a Galerkin system (cf. [9]), which is a matrix equation of order N of the form

$$(1.5) \qquad (I_N - K_N)\vec{f}_N = \vec{g}_N.$$

On the assumption that (1.1) has a unique solution, it can be proven that both $(I-T_N K)^{-1}$ and $(I_N-K_N)^{-1}$ exist for N large enough [9].

<u>EXAMPLE</u> (Piecewise linear interpolatory projections in C[0,1]).
Consider (1.1) - (1.2) in X = C[0,1]. Let Π_N: $0 = x_0 < x_1 < \ldots < x_N = 1$ be a regular grid on the interval [0,1]. Choose X_N to be the space of piecewise linear functions on Π_N spanned by $(u_0, u_1, \ldots, u_N)$ with:

$$u_0(x) = \begin{cases} (x-x_1)/(x_0-x_1) & , \quad x_0 \le x < x_1, \\ 0 & , \quad \text{elsewhere}, \end{cases}$$

$$u_N(x) = \begin{cases} (x-x_{N-1})/(x_N-x_{N-1}), & x_{N-1} \le x \le x_N, \\ 0 & , \quad \text{elsewhere}, \end{cases}$$

$$u_i(x) = \begin{cases} (x-x_{i-1})/(x_i-x_{i-1}), & x_{i-1} \le x < x_i, \\ (x-x_{i+1})/(x_i-x_{i+1}), & x_i \le x < x_{i+1}, \\ 0 & , \quad \text{elsewhere}, \end{cases}$$

for i = 1,...,N-1. For the projection operator T_N we choose the interpolatory operator defined by:

$$T_N f(x) = \sum_{i=0}^{N} f(x_i) u_i(x).$$

The Galerkin system reads

$$(1.6) \qquad (I_N - K_N) \begin{pmatrix} f_0 \\ \vdots \\ f_N \end{pmatrix} = \begin{pmatrix} g(x_0) \\ \vdots \\ g(x_N) \end{pmatrix},$$

where $(K_N)_{ij} = \int_0^1 k(x_i,y)u_j(y)dy$. The solution of (1.4) is given by the piecewise linear function taking the value f_i at x_i, $i = 0,\ldots,N$, where $\vec{f}_N$ is the solution of (1.6). For other examples of projection methods for Fredholm integral equations of the second kind we refer to IKEBE [9].

1.3. MULTIPLE GRID METHODS

The matrix K_N is in general a full matrix, i.e. all elements of K_N are non-zero. If N is small enough (1.5) can be solved by Gaussian elimination. For large values of N iterative methods are needed. In this thesis multiple grid methods are applied in order to solve the large non-sparse system (1.5) efficiently. These methods can be seen as an extension of the iterative schemes given by BRAKHAGE [5] and ATKINSON [3], who only use two grids (one coarse and one fine grid). Multiple grid methods work with a sequence of grids of increasing refinement, which are used simultaneously to obtain an approximation to (1.4), i.e. to compute efficiently the solution on the finest grid.

Let N_p, $p = 0,1,2,\ldots,\ell$, be an increasing sequence of integers ($N_0 < N_1 < \ldots < N_\ell$) and let X_p be a short notation for X_{N_p} (f_p, T_p and K_p are similarly defined). In the context of multiple grid iteration the subscript p is called *level*. We need the following assumption for $\{X_p\}$:

$$X_0 \subset X_1 \subset \ldots \subset X_\ell \subset X.$$

Suppose we want to solve (1.4) with $N = N_\ell$, i.e.:

$$(1.7) \qquad (I-T_\ell K)f_\ell = T_\ell g.$$

An approximation to f_ℓ is obtained by the following iterative process. Let the initial guess be zero, i.e. $f_\ell^{(0)} \equiv 0$. Perform the following steps for $i = 1(1)\sigma$:

$$(1.8a)\qquad f_\ell^{(i+\frac{1}{2})} = T_\ell K f_\ell^{(i)} + T_\ell g,$$

$$(1.8b)\qquad f_\ell^{(i+1)} = f_\ell^{(i+\frac{1}{2})} + T_\ell (I-T_{\ell-1}K)^{-1} T_{\ell-1}\{T_\ell g - f_\ell^{(i+\frac{1}{2})} + T_\ell K f_\ell^{(i+\frac{1}{2})}\}.$$

The first step (1.8a) of this scheme is a Jacobi or Picard iteration; the second step is called a *coarse grid correction*. As is shown in Chapter 2, the scheme (1.8) converges if $N_{\ell-1}$ is large enough. In order to understand the structure of (1.8b) we first consider the second part of the right-hand side. After (1.8a) the term between braces is equal to the residue of the Jacobi iteration:

$$r_\ell^{(i+\frac{1}{2})} \equiv T_\ell g - f_\ell^{(i+\frac{1}{2})} + T_\ell K f_\ell^{(i+\frac{1}{2})}.$$

This residue $r_\ell^{(i+\frac{1}{2})} \in X_\ell$ is projected to the subspace $X_{\ell-1}$ and we proceed with solving

$$(1.9)\qquad (I-T_{\ell-1}K)v_{\ell-1} = T_{\ell-1} r_\ell^{(i+\frac{1}{2})}.$$

We note that this equation is of the same type as (1.7), but all subscripts are decreased by 1. In a multiple grid method the solution of (1.9) is approximated by γ steps of the iterative process (1.8), except when it has to be solved on the lowest level. In that case the linear system corresponding to $(I-T_0K)v_0 = T_0 r_1^{(i+\frac{1}{2})}$ is solved by some direct method. In Chapter 2 it is shown that it is sufficient to take $\gamma = 2$ for the number of iterations.

The proposed multiple grid method to solve (1.7) is of a recursive type. Recursion takes place with respect to the level number p. For the precise description of a multiple grid algorithm the programming language ALGOL 68 [12] is convenient, because this language can easily handle both the recursion mentioned and the data structures that appear in a multiple grid algorithm. In order to describe our multiple grid method in a concise, modular and readable form we first introduce the following ALGOL-68 procedures in which *MODE VEC = REF [] REAL*.

```
PROC solve directly  = (VEC f,g) VOID:
                         # determines the solution of (I_p-K_p)f = g
                           by means of Gaussian-elimination #.

PROC zero            = (INT p) VEC:
                         # delivers the vector corresponding to
                           the zero-element of X_p #.

PROC restrict        = (VEC y_p) VEC:
                         # delivers the vector corresponding to T_p-1 y_p,
                           i.e. restrict is a representation of the
                           operator T_p-1: X_p → X_p-1 #.

PROC prolongate      = (VEC y_p) VEC:
                         # delivers the vector corresponding to T_p+1 y_p,
                           i.e. prolongate is a representation of the
                           operator T_p+1: X_p → X_p+1 #.
```

The following ALGOL 68 program describes our multiple grid process:

```
PROC mulgrid = (INT p,σ,VEC f,g) VOID:
IF p = 0
THEN solve directly (f,g)
ELSE TO σ
     DO f := g + K_p*f;
        VEC residue = g-f+K_p*f;
        VEC v := zero(p-1);
        mulgrid(p-1,γ,v,restrict(residue));
        f := f + prolongate (v)
     OD
FI;
```

The actual implementation of the procedures *zero*, *prolongate* and *restrict* depends on the choice of $\{X_p\}$ and the projection operators $\{T_p\}$. Using uniform grids and piecewise linear interpolatory projections in C[0,1], we give an implementation in Chapter 3. In [8] HACKBUSCH also studied the above multiple grid method for Fredholm integral equations of the second kind. In Chapter 2 we introduce an alternative multiple grid method, which can deal with a larger class of problems than the above method. The implementation of this new method is given in TEXT 3.3.2 (Chapter 3).

1.4. SCOPE OF THE STUDY

In this thesis we are concerned mainly with multiple grid methods for the fast solution of equations (1.4). In Chapter 2 various multiple grid methods are studied for these equations. For these iterative methods the reduction factors, which determine the rate of convergence, are derived using the collectively compact operator theory by ANSELONE [1] and ATKINSON [3]. Theoretical and numerical investigations show that multiple grid methods give the solution of (1.4) in $\mathcal{O}(N^2)$ operations as $N \to \infty$, whereas other iterative schemes take at least $\mathcal{O}(N^2 \log N)$ operations. In practice this results in algorithms for the solution of (1.4) that are significantly more efficient than the other schemes.

For the automatic solution of Fredholm integral equations of the second kind a new code, called *solve int eq* is presented in Chapter 3. The linear system obtained from the discretization of the integral equation is iteratively solved by a multiple grid method. For a variety of problems the performance of *solve int eq* is compared with Atkinson's program *iesimp* [2]. Using the number of kernel evaluations as a basis for comparison, the cost of the new algorithm is about 2/3 the cost of the algorithm *iesimp*; and it appears to be equally well or even more reliable.

In Chapter 4 we discuss the numerical solution of a two-dimensional Dirichlet problem for Laplace's equation. We use the classical approach of representation of the solution by means of a doublet distribution on the boundary of the domain. From the boundary condition we obtain a Fredholm integral equation of the second kind for the doublet distribution. We introduce a multiple grid method which makes use of a sequence of grids, that are generated by dividing the boundary into an increasing number of smaller and smaller panels. On these grids the doublet distribution is assumed to be constant over each panel. Assuming the boundary to satisfy a certain smoothness condition we prove that the reduction factor of the multiple grid process is less than $Ch^{1+\alpha}$, where h and α are a measure of the mesh-size and of the smoothness of the boundary, respectively. We illustrate this theoretical convergence result with the calculation of potential flow around a Kármán-Trefftz profile.

In Chapter 5 we deal with the nonlinear problem concerning the rotating flow due to an infinite disk performing torsional oscillations at an angular velocity Ω sin ωt. This problem is described by the Navier-Stokes and continuity equations. By means of the Von Kármán similarity transformations the equations are reduced to a nonlinear system of parabolic equations with periodic conditions in time. Applying these conditions we can reformulate the problem as a nonlinear operator equation of the type (1.3). This equation is solved by a multiple grid method.

This thesis is based on the following publications of the author:

[A] *Multiple grid methods for the solution of Fredholm integral equations of the second kind.*
This paper has been written jointly with P.W. Hemker and has been published in Mathematics of Computation 36 (1981), pp.215-232.
In fact, Chapter 2 of this thesis is an adapted version of this paper.

[B] *The automatic solution of Fredholm equations of the second kind.*
This paper will appear in the SIAM Journal on Scientific and Statistical Computing and is based on Chapter 3.

[C] *On the regularity of the principal value of the double layer potential.*
This paper contains the theoretical results of Section 4.1, which are applied to the aerodynamic problem of calculation of potential flow around 2-D bodies. It will appear in the Journal of Engineering Mathematics.

[D] *Analytical and numerical results for the non-stationary rotating disk flow.*
In this paper the analytical results of Section 5.2 and the finite difference schemes given in Section 5.3 have been published. It has appeared in the Journal of Engineering Mathematics 13 (1979), pp.173-191.

[E] *Application of multigrid methods for integral equations to two problems from fluid dynamics.*
This paper is based on Section 4.5 and Chapter 5. It was presented at the NASA-symposium "Multigrid methods", October 21-22, 1981, Moffett Field, California. It has been published in the NASA Conference Publication 2202.

REFERENCES TO CHAPTER 1

[1] ANSELONE, P.M., *Collectively compact operator approximation theory*, Prentice-Hall, Englewood Cliffs, N.J., 1971.

[2] ATKINSON, K.E., *An automatic program for linear Fredholm integral equations of the second kind*, ACM Transactions on Mathematical Software 2, 1976, pp.154-171.

[3] ATKINSON, K.E., *A survey of numerical methods for the solution of Fredholm integral equations of the second kind*, SIAM, Philadelphia, Pa., 1976.

[4] BERGER, M.S., *Nonlinearity and functional analysis*, Academic Press, New York, San Francisco, London, 1977.

[5] BRAKHAGE, H., *Über die numerische Behandlung von Integralgleichungen nach der Quadraturformelmethode*, Numerische Mathematik 2, 1960, pp.183-196.

[6] BREBBIA, C.A., Ed., *Recent advances in boundary element methods*, Pentech Press, London, Plymouth, 1978.

[7] BREBBIA, C.A., Ed., *New developments in boundary element methods*, CML Publications, Southampton, 1980.

[8] HACKBUSCH, W., *Die schnelle Auflösung der Fredholmschen Integralgleichung zweiter Art*, Beiträge zur Numerischen Mathematik 9, 1981, pp.47-62.

[9] IKEBE, Y., *The Galerkin method for the numerical solution of Fredholm integral equations of the second kind*, SIAM Review 14, 1972, pp.465-491.

[10] JASWON, M.A. & G.T. SYMM, *Integral equation methods in potential theory and elastostatics*, Academic Press, London, 1977.

[11] TE RIELE, H.J.J., Ed., *Colloquium Numerical treatment of integral equations*, MC-Syllabus 41, Mathematisch Centrum, Amsterdam, 1979.

[12] VAN WIJNGAARDEN, A. et al, Eds, *Revised report on the algorithmic language ALGOL 68*, Springer Verlag, New York, Heidelberg, Berlin, 1976.

CHAPTER 2

MULTIPLE GRID METHODS FOR THE SOLUTION OF FREDHOLM INTEGRAL EQUATIONS OF THE SECOND KIND

2.1. INTRODUCTION

Multiple grid methods have been advocated by BRANDT [5,6] for solving sparse systems of equations that arise from discretization of partial differential equations. Convergence and computational complexity of such multiple grid techniques have been studied since by HACKBUSCH [7,8] and WESSELING [12,13]. We intend to show that multiple grid methods can also be used advantageously for the non-sparse systems that occur in numerical methods for integral equations.

In [10] we have applied the multiple grid technique to the solution of Fredholm integral equations of the second kind

$$(2.1.1)\qquad f(x) - \int_0^1 k(x,y)f(y)dy = g(x), \qquad x \in [0,1],$$

where g belongs to a Banach space X. At the same time, HACKBUSCH [7] also used a multiple grid technique for these problems. Moreover, he gave a proof of convergence. In this proof he assumed the operator K, associated with the kernel $k(x,y)$ to map from X into a "smooth" subspace $\tilde{X} \subset X$, which has a stronger topology. In this chapter, for Hackbusch's method we give another proof, which fits into the theoretical framework developed by ANSELONE [1] and ATKINSON [2,3] for Fredholm equations. We assume that K is compact from X into X. In contrast to Hackbusch's analysis, this approach enables us to consider also Nyström interpolation as a permissible interpolation method. In addition, we introduce a new multiple grid method for Fredholm integral equations, which can deal with a larger class of problems than the method proposed by Hackbusch.

In 1978 STETTER [11] introduced the Defect Correction Principle for the formulation of various iterative methods. We shall apply this principle because it also appears to be an expedient tool to formulate multiple grid techniques.

In Section 2.2 we collect some results from papers by ATKINSON [2,3] and PRENTER [9]. In Section 2.3 we cast the iterative schemes of BRAKHAGE [4] and ATKINSON [2,3] into the context of the Defect Correction Principle and multiple grid iteration. Furthermore we give a proof of convergence of the multiple grid schemes with Nyström interpolation. In Section 2.4 we treat other interpolation methods and we extend the iterative schemes of Section 2.3 for subspaces X_p of X of finite dimension N_p. These schemes are used as a basis for the construction of a general algorithm for the solution of Fredholm equations of the second kind. This algorithm is more efficient than the algorithms by BRAKHAGE [4] and ATKINSON [2,3] because these schemes take $\mathcal{O}(N_p^3)$ and $\mathcal{O}(N_p^2 \log N_p)$ operations, respectively, whereas the multiple grid schemes result in $\mathcal{O}(N_p^2)$ operations. In Section 2.5 we illustrate the theoretical results of the previous sections by some numerical examples and we comment on the computational complexity.

2.2. BASIC ASSUMPTIONS AND RESULTS

Equation (2.1.1) can be written symbolically as

$$(2.2.1) \qquad Af = g, \qquad g \in X,$$

where X is a Banach space and $A = I - K$, with I the identity operator on X and K the linear operator associated with the kernel $k(x,y)$. A is assumed to have a bounded inverse on X. We shall discuss the convergence of a sequence of approximations to the unique solution of (2.2.1).

Let X_p, $p = 0,1,2,\ldots$, be finite-dimensional subspaces of X and let T_p, $p = 0,1,2,\ldots$, be a bounded projection operator from X onto X_p, i.e. $T_p f = f$ for all $f \in X_p$. We need the following assumptions for $\{X_p\}$ and $\{T_p\}$:

A1. $X_0 \subset X_1 \subset \ldots \subset X_p \subset \ldots \subset X$,

A2. $\lim_{p\to\infty} \| f - T_p f \| = 0$ for all $f \in X$.

<u>LEMMA 2.2.1</u>.

$$C_1 = \sup_{p\geq 0} \| T_p \| < \infty.$$

PROOF. The lemma follows from the principle of uniform boundedness, see ATKINSON [3], p.18. □

The sequence $\{X_p\}$ is thought to be associated with interpolating spline functions on a sequence of partitions $\{\Pi_p\}$ of the interval $[0,1]$ with mesh-sizes $\{h_p\}$. We assume that $h_p \to 0$ as $p \to \infty$. Corresponding with the sequence $\{\Pi_p\}$ we approximate K by a sequence of operators $\{K_p\}$, $K_p : X \to X$. Analogous to $A = I - K$, we also write $A_p = I - K_p$. In the context of multiple grid iteration, the subscript p is called *level*.

We use the following assumptions on K_p, $p = 0,1,2,\ldots,$

A3. K_p is a linear operator: $X \to X$.

A4. $\{K_p\}$ is a collectively compact family of operators, i.e., the set $S = \{K_p f \mid p \geq 0 \text{ and } \|f\| \leq 1\}$ has compact closure in X.

A5. $\lim_{p\to\infty} \|K_p f - Kf\| = 0$ for all $f \in X$.

A6. $K_p = K_p T_p$.

LEMMA 2.2.2. *From the Assumptions* A3 - A5 *follow:*

(i) K *is compact;*

(ii) *the sequence* $\{K_p\}$ *is uniformly bounded, i.e.* $C_2 = \sup_{p\geq 0} \|K_p\| < \infty$;

(iii) $\lim_{p\to\infty} \|(K-K_p)M\| = 0$ *for any compact operator* $M: X \to X$;

(iv) *let* $a_p = \sup_{q\geq p} \sup_{\ell\geq 0} \|(K-K_q)K_\ell\|$, *then* $\lim_{p\to\infty} a_p = 0$.

PROOF. See ATKINSON [3], p.96 and p.138. □

LEMMA 2.2.3. *Let the finite dimensional subspace* $X_0 \subset X$ *be sufficiently large (i.e. the mesh-width of the coarsest discretization is sufficiently small). From the existence of a bounded inverse of* $A = I - K$ *and the Assumptions* A3 - A5 *follow:*

(i) $(I-K_p)^{-1}$ *exists on* X *for* $p \geq 0$ *and* $C_3 = \sup_{p\geq 0} \|(I-K_p)^{-1}\| < \infty$;

(ii) $\|f-f_p\| \leq C_3 \|Kf-K_p f\|$, *where* f *is the solution of* (2.2.1) *and* f_p *of*

$$(2.2.2) \qquad (I-K_p)f_p = g.$$

PROOF. See ATKINSON [2], p.18. □

The following lemma is a summary of results given by PRENTER [9].

LEMMA 2.2.4. *From the Assumptions* A2 - A6 *follow:*

(i) *For any compact operator* M *on* X *into* X: $\lim_{p\to\infty} \|(I-T_p)M\| = 0$;

(ii) *if* X_0 *is sufficiently large, then* $(I-T_pK_p)^{-1}$ *exists on* X *for* $p \geq 0$ *and* $C_4 = \sup_{p\geq 0} \|(I-T_pK_p)^{-1}\| < \infty$.

Let $\tilde{f}_p$ be a solution of

$$(2.2.3) \qquad (I-T_pK_p)\tilde{f}_p = T_pg.$$

According to Lemma 2.2.4(ii), $\tilde{f}_p$ exists and is unique; it follows from (2.2.3) that $\tilde{f}_p \in X_p$.

LEMMA 2.2.5. *Let*

$$b_p = \sup_{q\geq p} \sup_{\ell\geq 0} \|(I-T_q)K_\ell\|,$$

then

$$\lim_{p\to\infty} b_p = 0.$$

PROOF. Let $\Psi = \{K_pf \mid p \geq 0 \text{ and } \|f\| < 1\}$. By Assumption A4, Ψ has compact closure in the Banach space X. Referring to Lemma 1 of ATKINSON [3], p.53, the convergence of T_pf is uniform on compact subsets of X. Then

$$\sup_{z\in\Psi} \|(I-T_q)z\| \to 0 \quad \text{for } q \to \infty$$

and therefore $b_p \to 0$ as $p \to \infty$. □

LEMMA 2.2.6. *Let the subspace* $X_0 \subset X$ *be sufficiently large; then*

$$\|\tilde{f}_p - T_pf\| \leq C_1C_4\|Kf-K_pf\|,$$

where f *is the solution of* (2.2.1).

PROOF. See PRENTER [9], Theorem 6.3. □

As a consequence of Assumption A1, the following lemma is trivial.

LEMMA 2.2.7. *Let* $q \leq p$, *i.e.* $\dim(X_q) \leq \dim(X_p)$; *then*

$$T_pT_q = T_q.$$

2.3. ITERATION SCHEMES WITH NYSTRÖM INTERPOLATION

In this section we use the Defect Correction Principle (cf. STETTER [11]) to formulate a class of iterative methods for the solution of (2.2.2). This equation is written as

$$(2.3.1) \qquad A_p f_p = g, \qquad g \in X,$$

with $A_p = I - K_p$. The Defect Correction Principle defines the following iterative process:

$$(2.3.2) \qquad \begin{cases} f_{p,0} = 0, \\ f_{p,i+1} = B_p g + (I-B_pA_p)f_{p,i}. \end{cases}$$

Here B_p denotes some approximate inverse of A_p, which is bijective and continuous in X. The solution f_p of (2.3.1) is a fixed point of (2.3.2) and (2.3.2) will converge to f_p if the reduction factor

$$\| I-B_pA_p \| < 1.$$

Several well-known iterative schemes for solving Fredholm integral equations of the second kind can be formulated within this framework. The iterative scheme of BRAKHAGE [4] is obtained by taking the following approximate inverse

$$(2.3.3) \qquad B_p^{(1)} = I + (I-K_{p-1})^{-1} K_p.$$

Here we notice that the operator $(I-K_q)^{-1}$, $q \geq 0$, as a mapping on X into X describes the process of discretization, solution of the discrete problem (i.e. the solution of a square linear system) and subsequent Nyström interpolation (see e.g. [10]). Other kinds of interpolation are treated in the next section.

The second iterative scheme of ATKINSON [2], p.19, arises from

$$(2.3.4) \qquad B_p^{(2)} = I + (I-K_0)^{-1} K_p.$$

The reduction factors of the corresponding iterative processes are estimated in the following theorem.

THEOREM 2.3.1.

(i) $\| I-B_p^{(1)}A_p \| \to 0$ *as* $p \to \infty$;

(ii) $\| I-B_p^{(2)}A_p \| \le C(X_0)$ *as* $p \to \infty$,

$C(X_0) < 1$ *for* X_0 *sufficiently large.*

PROOF. (i) Substitution of the explicit expressions for A_p and $B_p^{(1)}$ yields:

$$I - B_p^{(1)}A_p = I - \{I + (I-K_{p-1})^{-1} K_p\}(I-K_p) =$$

$$= K_p - (I-K_{p-1})^{-1} K_p(I-K_p) =$$

$$= (I-K_{p-1})^{-1}(K_p-K_{p-1})K_p.$$

From Lemmas 2.2.2 and 2.2.3 we get the following bound for the norm

$$\| (I-K_{p-1})^{-1}(K_p-K_{p-1})K_p \| \le C_3(a_p+a_{p-1}).$$

(ii) Analogously, we get for $B_p^{(2)}$ with X_0 sufficiently large,

$$\| I-B_p^{(2)}A_p \| \le C_3(a_p+a_0) \equiv C(X_0).$$

From Lemma 2.2.2 it follows that $C(X_0) < 1$ for all sufficiently large X_0. □

We remark that the approximate inverses $B_p^{(1)}$ and $B_p^{(2)}$ use only two levels: $B_p^{(1)}$ uses the levels p-1 and p, whereas $B_p^{(2)}$ uses the levels 0 and p. We now introduce approximate inverses $B_p^{(3)}$ and $B_p^{(4)}$, which use p+1 levels. They are defined recursively as follows:

$$(2.3.5)\qquad \begin{cases} B_0^{(3)} = (I-K_0)^{-1}, & \\ B_p^{(3)} = I + Q_{p-1}^{(3)}K_p, & p = 1,2,\ldots, \end{cases}$$

and

$$(2.3.6)\qquad \begin{cases} B_0^{(4)} = (I-K_0)^{-1}, & \\ B_p^{(4)} = Q_{p-1}^{(4)}(I-K_{p-1}+K_p), & p = 1,2,\ldots, \end{cases}$$

with $Q_p^{(j)}$, $j = 3,4$, $p = 0,1,2,\ldots$, given by

$$Q_p^{(j)} = \sum_{m=0}^{\gamma-1} (I-B_p^{(j)}A_p)^m B_p^{(j)}$$

for some positive integer γ. From the fact that $Q_p^{(j)}$ satisfies the equality

$$(I - Q_p^{(j)}A_p) = (I - B_p^{(j)}A_p)^{\gamma}$$

we see that $Q_p^{(j)}$ is an approximate inverse of A_p and its application is equivalent to the application of γ iteration steps of (2.3.2) with the use of the approximate inverse $B_p^{(j)}$. In fact, this is the motivation for this definition of $Q_p^{(j)}$ and it is the basis for the actual (recursive) implementation of the method.

In the following definition we give a short notation for the reduction factor for the various iterative processes.

DEFINITION.

$$\zeta_p^{(j)} = \| I-B_p^{(j)}A_p\|, \qquad j = 1,2,3,4.$$

THEOREM 2.3.2.

(i) $\zeta_p^{(3)} \le \zeta_p^{(1)} + \zeta_{p-1}^{(3)\gamma}(\zeta_p^{(1)} + \|K_p\|)$,

(ii) $\zeta_p^{(4)} \le \zeta_p^{(1)} + \zeta_{p-1}^{(4)\gamma}(\zeta_p^{(1)} + 1)$.

PROOF. (i) By definition

$$I - B_p^{(1)} A_p = I - \{I + A_{p-1}^{-1}(I-A_p)\}A_p$$

and

$$I - B_p^{(3)} A_p = I - \{I + [I - (I - B_{p-1}^{(3)}A_{p-1})^{\gamma}]A_{p-1}^{-1}(I - A_p)\}A_p =$$

$$= I - B_p^{(1)}A_p + (I - B_{p-1}^{(3)}A_{p-1})^{\gamma}A_{p-1}^{-1}(I - A_p)A_p =$$

$$= I - B_p^{(1)}A_p + (I - B_{p-1}^{(3)}A_{p-1})^{\gamma}(B_p^{(1)} - I)A_p.$$

Hence

$$\|I - B_p^{(3)}A_p\| \le \|I - B_p^{(1)}A_p\| + \|I - B_{p-1}^{(3)}A_{p-1}\|^{\gamma}\{\|I - B_p^{(1)}A_p\| + \|I - A_p\|\},$$

i.e.

$$\zeta_p^{(3)} \le \zeta_p^{(1)} + \zeta_{p-1}^{(3)\gamma}(\zeta_p^{(1)} + \|K_p\|).$$

(ii) Similar to the case (i). Now we have

$$I - B_p^{(4)} A_p = I - [I - (I - B_{p-1}^{(4)} A_{p-1})^\gamma] A_{p-1}^{-1} (A_{p-1} - A_p + I) A_p =$$

$$= I - B_p^{(1)} A_p + (I - B_{p-1}^{(4)} A_{p-1})^\gamma B_p^{(1)} A_p.$$

Hence

$$\| I - B_p^{(4)} A_p \| \le \| I - B_p^{(1)} A_p \| + \| I - B_{p-1}^{(4)} A_{p-1} \|^\gamma \| I - B_p^{(1)} A_p - I \|,$$

i.e.

$$\zeta_p^{(4)} \le \zeta_p^{(1)} + \zeta_{p-1}^{(4)\,\gamma} (\zeta_p^{(1)} + 1). \qquad \square$$

By Theorem 2.3.1 we know that $\zeta_p^{(1)} \to 0$ as $p \to \infty$; conditions for $\zeta_p^{(3)}$ to vanish depend on γ, $\|K_p\|$ and $\zeta_p^{(1)}$, whereas the conditions for $\zeta_p^{(4)}$ depend on γ and $\zeta_p^{(1)}$ only. In order to study this dependence further we prove the following lemma.

LEMMA 2.3.3. *Let* $k \in \mathbb{R}$ *and* $\gamma \in \mathbb{N}$ *be given, let* $\{v_p \mid v_p > 0,\ p = 1,2,\ldots\}$ *be a non-increasing sequence with* $d = \inf_p \frac{v_p}{v_{p-1}}$ *and let* $\{w_p\}$ *be defined by*

$$\begin{cases} w_1 = v_1 \\ w_p = v_p + w_{p-1}^\gamma (v_p + k). \end{cases}$$

If either

$$\text{(i)} \quad \begin{cases} \gamma \ge 1, & 0 < k < d < 1 \text{ and} \\ v_1 < \tfrac{1}{2}(1 - \tfrac{k}{d}), \end{cases}$$

or

$$\text{(ii)} \quad \begin{cases} \gamma \ge 2 & \text{and} \\ v_1 < \tfrac{1}{2}\{\sqrt{1 + (\tfrac{k}{d})^2} - \tfrac{k}{d}\}, \end{cases}$$

then a $C > 0$ *exists such that* $v_p \le w_p \le C v_p$.

PROOF. (i) We define $c = \frac{d+k}{d-k}$; then $c > 1$ and the conditions on $\{v_p\}$ are written as

$$(2.3.7) \qquad k\,\frac{c+1}{c-1} < \frac{v_p}{v_{p-1}} \le 1$$

and

(2.3.8) $\quad (1+c)v_1 < 1.$

We show that the lemma is true for $C = 1+c$. From (2.3.8) we see $w_1 = v_1 < (1+c)v_1 < 1$. Now we show by induction that $w_p < (1+c)v_p < 1$ assuming that $w_{p-1} < (1+c)v_{p-1} < 1$. From (2.3.7) follows

$$\frac{v_{p-1}}{v_p} k < \frac{c-1}{c+1}, \quad \left(\frac{1}{c+1} + \frac{v_{p-1}}{v_p}k\right) < \frac{c}{c+1},$$

$$(1+c)^{\gamma-1}\, v_{p-1}^{\gamma-1}\left(v_{p-1} + \frac{v_{p-1}}{v_p} k\right) < \frac{c}{c+1},$$

$$w_{p-1}^{\gamma}(v_p+k) < (1+c)^{\gamma} v_{p-1}^{\gamma}(v_p+k) < cv_p,$$

$$w_p = v_p + w_{p-1}^{\gamma}(v_p+k) < (1+c)v_p.$$

(ii) We assume $v_1 < \sqrt{(\frac{k}{2d})^2 + \frac{c}{(1+c)^2}} - \frac{k}{2d}$ for some $0 < c \leq 1$ and we show $w_p \leq (1+c)v_p$; then the lemma is proven by taking $c = 1$. For any $v \in [0,v_1]$ we have

$$v^2 + \frac{k}{d} v - \frac{c}{(1+c)^2} < 0.$$

Hence $(1+c)v(v + \frac{k}{d}) < \frac{c}{1+c}$. By assumption we know

$$w_1 = v_1 < (1+c)v_1 < \sqrt{\{\frac{k(1+c)}{2d}\}^2 + c} - \frac{k(1+c)}{2d} < \sqrt{c} \leq 1.$$

Now we show by induction that $w_p < (1+c)v_p < 1$, assuming that $w_{p-1} < (1+c)v_{p-1} < 1$:

$$(1+c)v_{p-1}(v_{p-1} + \frac{k}{d}) < \frac{c}{1+c},$$

$$(1+c)v_{p-1}\left(v_{p-1} + \frac{v_{p-1}}{v_p} k\right) < \frac{c}{1+c},$$

$$(1+c)^2 v_{p-1}^2\left(1 + \frac{k}{v_p}\right) < c,$$

$$(1+c)^{\gamma} v_{p-1}^{\gamma}\left(1 + \frac{k}{v_p}\right) < c, \qquad \gamma = 2,3,\ldots,$$

$$w_{p-1}^{\gamma}\left(1+\frac{k}{v_p}\right) < c,$$

$$w_p = v_p + w_{p-1}^{\gamma}(v_p+k) < (1+c)v_p. \qquad \square$$

THEOREM 2.3.4. *Let* $\gamma \geq 2$ *and let* $\zeta_p^{(1)}$ *satisfy*

$$\zeta_p^{(1)} \leq v_p = d^{p-1}v_1$$

for some $0 < d < 1$. *Then*

(i) *if* $v_1 \leq \frac{1}{2d}\{\sqrt{d^2+C_2^2} - C_2\}$ *with* C_2 *as defined in Lemma* 2.2.2, *it follows that* $\zeta_p^{(3)} \leq 2v_p$, *and*

(ii) *if* $v_1 \leq \frac{1}{2d}\{\sqrt{1+d^2} - 1\}$ *it follows that* $\zeta_p^{(4)} \leq 2v_p$.

PROOF. (i) Let $\{w_p\}$be defined as in Lemma 2.3.3 with $k = C_2 = \sup_{p\geq 0}\|K_p\|$, then it follows from the proof of Lemma 2.3.3 that

$$w_p \leq 2v_p,$$

Therefore we show $\zeta_p^{(3)} \leq w_p$ by induction: from the definition of $\zeta_p^{(3)}$ we derive

$$\zeta_1^{(3)} = \zeta_1^{(1)} \leq v_1 = w_1$$

and by Theorem 2.3.2

$$\zeta_p^{(3)} \leq \zeta_p^{(1)} + \zeta_{p-1}^{(3)\,\gamma}(\zeta_p^{(1)} + \|K_p\|) \leq v_p + w_{p-1}^{\gamma}(v_p + C_2) = w_p.$$

(ii) Similarly, with $\{w_p\}$ defined as in Lemma 2.3.3 with $k = 1$, we prove $\zeta_p^{(4)} < w_p$ and hence

$$\zeta_p^{(4)} < w_p < 2v_p. \qquad \square$$

REMARK. If $B_p^{(3)}$ is defined with $\gamma = 1$, then a similar proof yields that, for any decreasing sequence $\{v_p\}$ with

$$\sup_{p\geq 0}\|K_p\| = C_2 < d = \inf_p \frac{v_p}{v_{p-1}} < 1,$$

for which

$$\zeta_p^{(1)} \le v_p,$$

we have

$$\zeta_p^{(3)} < \frac{2d}{d - C_2} v_p. \qquad \square$$

By $f_{p,\sigma}^{(j)}$ we denote the result of σ applications of the Defect Correction Process on level p with approximate inverse $B_p^{(j)}$, $j = 3,4$, when we take zero as the initial approximant.

With the aid of the previous theorem and Lemma 2.2.3 the following theorem is immediate.

THEOREM 2.3.5 (Approximation theorem). *Under the hypotheses of Theorem* 2.3.4 *the multiple grid process yields approximate solutions for which the following error estimate holds:*

$$\| f - f_{p,\sigma}^{(j)} \| \le C_3 \| K_p f - K f \| + (2d^{p-1} v_1)^{\sigma} \| f_p \|, \qquad j = 3,4,$$

where f *and* f_p *are the solutions of* (2.2.1) *and* (2.2.2), *respectively.*

PROOF. The proof follows immediately from

$$\| f - f_{p,\sigma}^{(j)} \| \le \| f - f_p \| + \| f_p - f_{p,\sigma}^{(j)} \|. \qquad \square$$

2.4. ITERATION SCHEMES WITH PROJECTION INTO FINITE DIMENSIONAL SUBSPACES

In this section we expand the technique used in Section 2.3 to find the solution in X_p of the equation (2.2.3):

$$(2.4.1) \qquad \tilde{A}_p \tilde{f}_p = g_p, \qquad g_p \in X_p,$$

where $\tilde{A}_p = I - T_p K_p$ is a mapping on X into X. We assume that X_0 is sufficiently large such that $(I - T_p K_p)^{-1}$ exists for all $p \ge 0$.

Analogous to the approximate inverse of A_p in the previous section, we now introduce:

$$\tilde{B}_p^{(1)} = I + T_p\tilde{A}_{p-1}^{-1}T_{p-1}T_pK_p,$$

$$\tilde{B}_p^{(2)} = I + T_p\tilde{A}_0^{-1}T_0T_pK_p,$$

$$\begin{cases} \tilde{B}_0^{(3)} = \tilde{A}_0^{-1}T_0, \\ \tilde{B}_p^{(3)} = I + T_p\tilde{Q}_{p-1}^{(3)}T_{p-1}T_pK_p, \end{cases}$$

$$\begin{cases} \tilde{B}_0^{(4)} = \tilde{A}_0^{-1}T_0, \\ \tilde{B}_p^{(4)} = I - T_pT_{p-1}T_p + T_pQ_{p-1}^{(4)}T_{p-1}(I - K_{p-1} + T_pK_p)T_p, \end{cases}$$

with

$$\tilde{Q}_p^{(j)} = \sum_{m=0}^{\gamma-1} (I - \tilde{B}_p^{(j)}\tilde{A}_p)^m\tilde{B}_p^{(j)}, \quad j = 3,4,$$

for some positive integer γ.

The operators $\tilde{B}_p^{(j)}$, $j = 1,2,3,4$, are all mappings on X into X. The solution $\tilde{f}_p \in X_p$ of (2.4.1) is approximated by a defect correction process of the form

$$\text{(2.4.2)} \qquad \begin{cases} \tilde{f}_{p,0} = 0, \\ \tilde{f}_{p,i+1} = \tilde{B}_pg_p + (I - \tilde{B}_p\tilde{A}_p)\tilde{f}_{p,i}. \end{cases}$$

We notice that $\tilde{B}_p^{(1)}$ and $\tilde{B}_p^{(3)}$ yield iterative processes that are equivalent respectively with the "One Step Method" and the "Multi Grid Method" discussed in HACKBUSCH [7]. $\tilde{B}_p^{(2)}$ yields an iterative process analogous to Atkinson's method, whereas $\tilde{B}_p^{(4)}$ yields a new multiple grid method with better convergence properties than $\tilde{B}_p^{(3)}$.

Analogously to Section 2.3, but restricting the domain of the operators to X_p, we see that here $\tilde{Q}_p^{(j)}: X_p \to X_p$ is an approximate inverse of $\tilde{A}_p: X_p \to X_p$ and the amplification operator on X_p into X_p of a defect correction step with $\tilde{Q}_p^{(j)}$ is

$$I - \tilde{Q}_p^{(j)}\tilde{A}_p = (I - \tilde{B}_p^{(j)}\tilde{A}_p)^\gamma.$$

Thus, one application of $\tilde{Q}_p^{(j)}$ is equivalent with the γ times application of

$\tilde{B}_p^{(j)}$ and we may write

$$\tilde{Q}_p^{(j)} = [I - (I - \tilde{B}_p^{(j)}\tilde{A}_p)^{\gamma}]\tilde{A}_p^{-1}.$$

The convergence of the process (2.4.2) depends on the Lipschitz constant of the operator $I - \tilde{B}_p\tilde{A}_p$ as a mapping $X_p \to X_p$. Therefore its reduction factor is given by

$$\| T_p(I - \tilde{B}_p\tilde{A}_p)\| .$$

This reduction factor is studied in the remainder of this section.

<u>THEOREM 2.4.1.</u>
(i) $\| T_p(I-\tilde{B}_p^{(1)}\tilde{A}_p)\| \to 0$ *as* $p \to \infty$;
(ii) $\| T_p(I-\tilde{B}_p^{(2)}\tilde{A}_p)\| \leq \tilde{C}(X_0)$ *as* $p \to \infty$, $\tilde{C}(X_0) < 1$ *for* X_0 *sufficiently large.*

<u>PROOF</u>. (i) Substitution of the explicit expressions for $\tilde{B}_p^{(1)}$ and $\tilde{A}_p$ yields, with $\ell = p-1$:

$$T_p(I - \tilde{B}_p^{(1)}\tilde{A}_p) = T_p\tilde{A}_\ell^{-1}\{\tilde{A}_\ell - T_\ell T_p \tilde{A}_p\}K_p.$$

The expression between braces is rewritten as

$$\{I-T_\ell+T_\ell(I-T_p+T_pK_p-K_\ell)\}.$$

Therefore we have

$$\| T_p(I - \tilde{B}_p^{(1)}A_p)\| \leq$$

$$\leq \| T_p\| \| \tilde{A}_\ell^{-1}\| [\| (I-T_\ell)K_p\| +$$

$$+ \| T_\ell\| \{\| (I-T_p)K_p\| + \| (I-T_p)K_\ell\| \| K_p\| +$$

$$+ \| T_p\| \| (K_p-K)K_p\| + \| T_p\| \| (K-K_\ell)K_p\| \}].$$

Using the lemmas 2.2.1 to 2.2.5 we obtain the proof of (i) by the same arguments as used for the proof of lemma 2.3.1.

(ii) Replace the subscript ℓ by 0 in the first part of the proof. For

$p \to \infty$, $\|(I-T_p)K_p\|$, $\|(I-T_p)K_0\|$ and $\|(K_p-K)K_p\|$ vanish, whereas the other terms tend to a constant value depending on X_0. □

DEFINITION. $\eta_p^{(j)} = \|T_p(I - \tilde{B}_p^{(j)}\tilde{A}_p)\|$, $j = 1,2,3,4$.

THEOREM 2.4.2.

(i) $\eta_p^{(3)} < \eta_p^{(1)} + \eta_{p-1}^{(3)^\gamma}[\eta_p^{(1)} + \|T_p\|\|K_p\|]$;

(ii) $\eta_p^{(4)} < \eta_p^{(1)} + \eta_{p-1}^{(4)^\gamma}[\eta_p^{(1)} + \|T_p\|]$.

PROOF. We use the notation $M_p^{(j)} = I - \tilde{B}_p^{(j)}\tilde{A}_p$, $j = 1,3,4$. From Assumption A6 and the definitions of $\tilde{A}_p$ and $\tilde{B}_p^{(j)}$, $j = 1,3,4$, it is clear that:

$$T_p\tilde{A}_p = \tilde{A}_pT_p,$$

and

$$T_p\tilde{B}_p^{(j)} = \tilde{B}_p^{(j)}T_p, \quad j = 1,3,4.$$

Hence

$$T_pM_p^{(j)} = M_p^{(j)}T_p, \quad j = 1,3,4,$$

and also

$$\tilde{Q}_p^{(j)} = [I - M_p^{(j)^\gamma}]\tilde{A}_p^{-1}.$$

(i) From the definition of $\tilde{B}_p^{(1)}$ we get, with $\ell = p-1$:

$$M_p^{(1)} = I - \tilde{A}_p - T_p\tilde{A}_\ell^{-1}T_\ell T_pK_p\tilde{A}_p = T_pK_p - T_p\tilde{A}_\ell^{-1}T_\ell T_pK_p\tilde{A}_p.$$

Use lemma 2.2.7 and the relation $\tilde{A}_\ell^{-1}T_\ell = T_\ell\tilde{A}_\ell^{-1}$ to prove that

$$M_p^{(1)} = T_pK_p - \tilde{A}_\ell^{-1}T_\ell T_pK_p\tilde{A}_p.$$

These relations are used to prove that

$$\begin{aligned} M_p^{(3)} &= I - \{I + T_p(I-M_\ell^{(3)^\gamma})\tilde{A}_\ell^{-1}T_\ell T_pK_p\}\tilde{A}_p = \\ &= M_p^{(1)} + T_pM_\ell^{(3)^\gamma}\tilde{A}_\ell^{-1}T_\ell T_pK_p\tilde{A}_p = \\ &= M_p^{(1)} + T_pM_\ell^{(3)^\gamma}(T_pK_p - M_p^{(1)}). \end{aligned}$$

It is easily verified that $M_p^{(1)} = T_p M_p^{(1)}$ and $M_p^{(3)} = T_p M_p^{(3)}$. By means of Lemma 2.2.7 we get

$$M_p^{(3)} = M_p^{(1)} + M_\ell^{(3)^\gamma}(T_p K_p - M_p^{(1)}).$$

Hence

$$\eta_p^{(3)} \le \eta_p^{(1)} + \eta_{p-1}^{(3)^\gamma}(\eta_p^{(1)} + \|T_p\|\|K_p\|).$$

(ii) $$M_p^{(4)} = I - \{I - T_p T_\ell T_p + T_p(I - M_\ell^{(4)^\gamma})\tilde{A}_\ell^{-1} T_\ell(\tilde{A}_\ell + T_p K_p)T_p\}\tilde{A}_p =$$

$$= M_p^{(1)} + T_p M_\ell^{(4)^\gamma} T_\ell(I + \tilde{A}_\ell^{-1} T_\ell T_p K_p)\tilde{A}_p T_p.$$

From this expression we conclude that $M_p^{(4)} = T_p M_p^{(4)} = M_p^{(4)} T_p$. Using Lemma 2.2.7 we obtain $T_p M_\ell^{(4)} = M_\ell^{(4)}$ and

$$M_p^{(4)} = M_p^{(1)} + M_\ell^{(4)^\gamma}(I - M_p^{(1)})T_p.$$

Hence

$$\eta_p^{(4)} \le \eta_p^{(1)} + \eta_{p-1}^{(4)^\gamma}(\eta_p^{(1)} + \|T_p\|). \qquad \square$$

THEOREM 2.4.3. *Let* $\gamma \ge 2$ *and let* $\eta_p^{(1)}$ *satisfy* $\eta_p^{(1)} \le v_p = d^{p-1}v_1$, *for some* $0 < d < 1$; *then*

(i) *if* $v_1 \le \frac{1}{2d}\{\sqrt{d^2+C_1^2C_2^2} - C_1C_2\}$, *it follows that* $\eta_p^{(3)} \le 2v_p$, *and*

(ii) *if* $v_1 \le \frac{1}{2d}\{\sqrt{d^2+C_1^2} - C_1\}$, *it follows that* $\eta_p^{(4)} \le 2v_p$,
where C_1 *and* C_2 *are defined as in Section* 2.2.

PROOF. (i) Use Lemma 2.3.3 with $k = C_1C_2$ and Theorem 2.4.2.

(ii) Analogously with $k = C_1$. $\square$

By $\tilde{f}_{p,\sigma}^{(j)}$ we denote the result of σ applications of the Defect Correction Process on level p with approximate inverse $\tilde{B}_p^{(j)}$, j = 1,3,4, when we take zero as the initial approximant.

THEOREM 2.4.4 (Approximation theorem). *Under the hypotheses of Theorem* 2.4.3 *the multiple grid process yields* $\tilde{f}_{p,\sigma}^{(j)}$, *for which the following error estimates hold:*

$$\|f - \tilde{f}_{p,\sigma}^{(j)}\| \le \|f - T_p f\| + C_1C_4\|Kf - K_p f\| + (2d^{p-1}v_1)^\sigma \|\tilde{f}_p\|,$$

where f *and* $\tilde{f}_p$ *are the solutions of* (2.2.1) *and* (2.2.3), *respectively.*

PROOF. For j = 1,3,4 we have

$$\|f-\tilde{f}_{p,\sigma}^{(j)}\| \le \|f-T_pf\| + \|T_pf-\tilde{f}_p\| + \|\tilde{f}_p-\tilde{f}_{p,\sigma}^{(j)}\|$$

and the proof follows from Lemma 2.2.6 and Theorem 2.4.3. □

We notice that the usual discretization methods easily satisfy the first condition of Theorem 2.4.3 as is illustrated in Section 2.5. The other condition of Theorem 2.4.3, which requires an upperbound on v_1, is essentially a requirement on the coarsest discretization used in the multiple grid algorithm. This condition is also discussed in the next section.

2.5. NUMERICAL RESULTS

In this section we illustrate the theoretical convergence results from the previous sections and we make some remarks about the computational complexity of the various methods. We shall only show numerical results obtained with the methods that appear to be the most efficient. These methods are defined by the approximate inverses $B_p^{(2)}$ (Atkinson's method), $\tilde{B}_p^{(3)}$ (Hackbusch's method) and $\tilde{B}_p^{(4)}$ (a new method with better convergence properties).

As an example, the integral equation

$$(2.5.1) \qquad f(x) - \lambda \int_0^1 \cos(\pi xy) f(y)\,dy = g(x)$$

is solved for various values of the parameter λ (cf. HACKBUSCH [7] who gives results for the same equation); g(x) is chosen such that

$$f(x) = e^x \cos(7x).$$

The operators K_p are defined by means of the repeated trapezoidal rule:

$$K_p f(x) = \sum_{j=0}^{N_p} w_j k(x,x_j) f(x_j),$$

where the nodal points $\{x_j\}$ are uniformly distributed ($x_0 = 0$, $x_{N_p} = 1$ and the weights $\{w_j\}$ are given by $\{\frac{1}{2}h_p, h_p, h_p, \ldots, h_p, \frac{1}{2}h_p\}$, with $h_p = (N_p)^{-1}$. The projection operators are defined by piecewise linear interpolation at the nodal points $\{x_j\}$. The various grid-levels are related by $N_p = 2N_{p-1}$.

For the operators $\{K_p\}$ and $\{T_p\}$ we know (cf. ATKINSON [3] and PRENTER [9]) that, if f is the solution of (2.5.1):

(2.5.2) $\qquad \|K_p f - Kf\| = \mathcal{O}(h_p^2),$

(2.5.3) $\qquad \|T_p f - f\| = \mathcal{O}(h_p^2),$

(2.5.4) $\qquad a_p = \mathcal{O}(h_p^2)$

and

(2.5.5) $\qquad b_p = \mathcal{O}(h_p^2) \quad$ for $p \to \infty$,

with a_p and b_p defined as in Lemmas 2.2.2 and 2.2.5, respectively. Using these estimates, we easily derive (see the proof of Theorem 2.4.1)

$$\eta_p^{(1)} \le v_p = Ch_{p-1}^2.$$

Because the successive mesh-sizes are related by $h_p = h_0 2^{-p}$ we have

(2.5.6) $\qquad \eta_p^{(1)} \le v_p = 4Ch_0^2 4^{-p}.$

Comparing this expression with the assumption on $\eta_p^{(1)}$ in Theorem 2.4.3 we see that $d = 1/4$. In the same theorem conditions on $\eta_1^{(1)}$ are formulated for the multiple grid methods to converge. Comparing these conditions we conclude that the condition on $\eta_1^{(1)}$ in the process defined by $\tilde{B}_p^{(4)}$ is independent of $C_2 = \sup_{p\ge 0} \|K_p\|$, whereas in the process defined by $\tilde{B}_p^{(3)}$ the condition on $\eta_1^{(1)}$ becomes stronger as $\sup_{p\ge 0} \|K_p\|$ increases. In Figure 2.1 we sketch the regions of convergence induced by $\tilde{B}_p^{(3)}$ and $\tilde{B}_p^{(4)}$ as derived from Theorem 2.4.3 with $d = 1/4$ and $\gamma = 2$.

Hence, from Theorem 2.4.3 one may expect that both multiple grid methods yield similar results as $\|K\| \approx 1$ whereas they differ for $\|K\| \gg 1$. For the integral equation (2.5.1) $\|K\| \gg 1$ holds for $\lambda \gg 1$.

In Tables 2.5.1 - 2.5.3 we give the observed reduction factor

$$\eta(N_p;N_0) = [\|\tilde{f}_{p,i+1} - \tilde{f}_{p,i}\| / \|\tilde{f}_{p,1} - \tilde{f}_{p,0}\|]^{1/i},$$

for the iterative methods defined by $B_p^{(2)}$, $\tilde{B}_p^{(3)}$ and $\tilde{B}_p^{(4)}$, respectively,

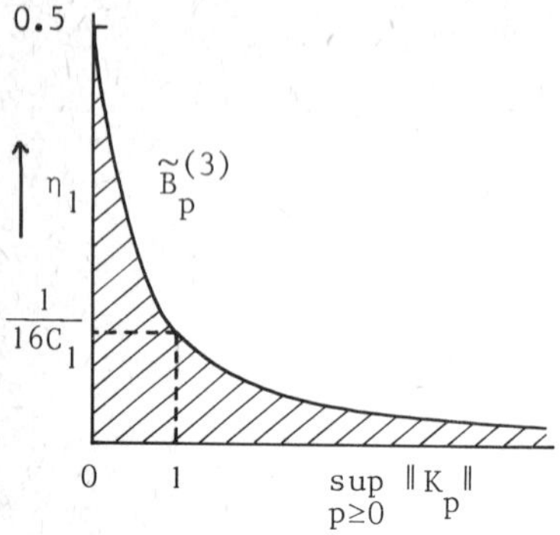

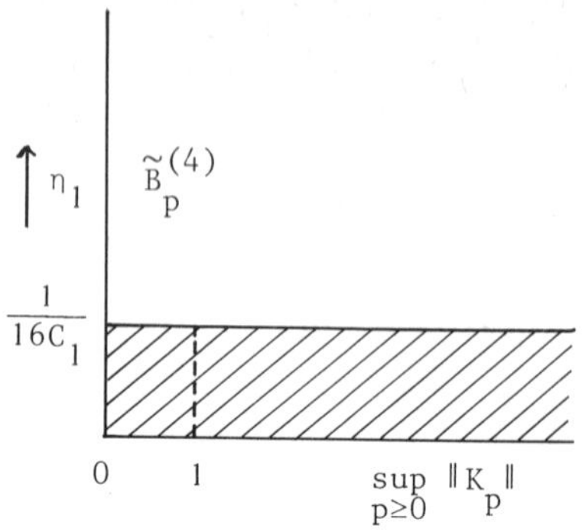

Figure 2.1. The multiple grid convergence regions. The coarsest grid reduction factor η_1 versus $C_2 = \sup_{p\geq 0} \|K_p\|$; $C_1 = \sup_{p\geq 0} \|T_p\|$.

with $\gamma = 2$. The dependence of $\eta(N_p;N_0)$ on N_p, the number of mesh intervals in the finest grid, and on N_0, the number in the coarsest grid, is shown. The value of i is suitably chosen and $\|\cdot\|$ denotes the maximum norm. From Table 2.5.1 we see that the reduction factors of Atkinson's method tend to a constant value as $N_p \to \infty$. As was expected, it decreases as N_0 increases.

In the case of convergence, the Tables 2.5.2 and 2.5.3 asymptotically show similar results. However for larger values of λ the new multiple grid method needs fewer subintervals in the coarsest grid. The quotients $\eta(N_p;N_0)/\eta(N_{p-1};N_0)$ approximate the value $d = 1/4$, which is in agreement with the theory.

λ	N_p \ N_0	2	4	8	16	32	64
1	4	$.23\ 10^{-1}$					
	8	$.28\ 10^{-1}$	$.58\ 10^{-2}$				
	16	$.30\ 10^{-1}$	$.72\ 10^{-2}$	$.15\ 10^{-2}$			
	32	$.30\ 10^{-1}$	$.76\ 10^{-2}$	$.18\ 10^{-2}$	$.38\ 10^{-3}$		
	64	$.30\ 10^{-1}$	$.78\ 10^{-2}$	$.19\ 10^{-2}$	$.47\ 10^{-3}$	$.83\ 10^{-4}$	
	128	$.30\ 10^{-1}$	$.78\ 10^{-2}$	$.19\ 10^{-2}$	$.52\ 10^{-3}$	$.10\ 10^{-3}$	$.24\ 10^{-4}$
10	4	$.11\ 10^{+1}$					
	8	$.16\ 10^{+1}$	$.18\ 10^{0}$				
	16	$.17\ 10^{+1}$	$.22\ 10^{0}$	$.36\ 10^{-1}$			
	32	$.17\ 10^{+1}$	$.23\ 10^{0}$	$.45\ 10^{-1}$	$.86\ 10^{-2}$		
	64	$.17\ 10^{+1}$	$.24\ 10^{0}$	$.48\ 10^{-1}$	$.11\ 10^{-1}$	$.21\ 10^{-2}$	
	128	$.17\ 10^{+1}$	$.24\ 10^{0}$	$.48\ 10^{-1}$	$.11\ 10^{-1}$	$.27\ 10^{-2}$	$.38\ 10^{-3}$
100	4	$.64\ 10^{+1}$					
	8	$.11\ 10^{+2}$	$.14\ 10^{+1}$				
	16	$.14\ 10^{+2}$	$.16\ 10^{+1}$	$.40\ 10^{0}$			
	32	$.15\ 10^{+2}$	$.16\ 10^{+1}$	$.42\ 10^{0}$	$.99\ 10^{-1}$		
	64	$.15\ 10^{+2}$	$.16\ 10^{+1}$	$.45\ 10^{0}$	$.15\ 10^{0}$	$.33\ 10^{-1}$	
	128	$.15\ 10^{+2}$	$.16\ 10^{+1}$	$.49\ 10^{0}$	$.16\ 10^{0}$	$.41\ 10^{-1}$	$.68\ 10^{-2}$

Table 2.5.1. Reduction factors for the two-grid method defined by $B_p^{(2)}$ (Atkinson's method).

λ	N_p \ N_0	2	4	8	16	32	64
1	4	$.31\ 10^{-1}$					
	8	$.98\ 10^{-2}$	$.94\ 10^{-2}$				
	16	$.24\ 10^{-2}$	$.24\ 10^{-2}$	$.23\ 10^{-2}$			
	32	$.62\ 10^{-3}$	$.62\ 10^{-3}$	$.62\ 10^{-3}$	$.62\ 10^{-3}$		
	64	$.14\ 10^{-3}$	$.14\ 10^{-3}$	$.14\ 10^{-3}$	$.14\ 10^{-3}$	$.14\ 10^{-3}$	
	128	$.35\ 10^{-4}$	$.35\ 10^{-4}$	$.35\ 10^{-4}$	$.35\ 10^{-4}$	$.34\ 10^{-4}$	$.35\ 10^{-4}$
10	4	$.32\ 10^{0}$					
	8	$.12\ 10^{+1}$	$.10\ 10^{0}$				
	16	$.42\ 10^{+1}$	$.12\ 10^{0}$	$.25\ 10^{-1}$			
	32	$.20\ 10^{+3}$	$.18\ 10^{-1}$	$.13\ 10^{-1}$	$.62\ 10^{-2}$		
	64	$.23\ 10^{+6}$	$.91\ 10^{-2}$	$.24\ 10^{-2}$	$.23\ 10^{-2}$	$.19\ 10^{-2}$	
	128	$.40\ 10^{+12}$	$.46\ 10^{-3}$	$.57\ 10^{-3}$	$.52\ 10^{-3}$	$.53\ 10^{-3}$	$.51\ 10^{-3}$
100	4	$.43\ 10^{+1}$					
	8	$.11\ 10^{+4}$	$.11\ 10^{+1}$				
	16	$.66\ 10^{+7}$	$.77\ 10^{+2}$	$.29\ 10^{0}$			
	32	$.17\ 10^{+17}$	$.79\ 10^{+4}$	$.51\ 10^{+1}$	$.10\ 10^{0}$		
	64	$.82\ 10^{+34}$	$.46\ 10^{+11}$	$.15\ 10^{+3}$	$.33\ 10^{0}$	$.29\ 10^{-1}$	
	128	$.80\ 10^{+70}$	$.86\ 10^{+23}$	$.96\ 10^{+7}$	$.43\ 10^{0}$	$.24\ 10^{-1}$	$.85\ 10^{-2}$

Table 2.5.2. Reduction factors for the multiple grid method defined by $\tilde{B}_p^{(3)}$ (Hackbusch's method).

λ	N_p \ N_0	2	4	8	16	32	64
1	4	$.31\ 10^{-1}$					
	8	$.95\ 10^{-2}$	$.94\ 10^{-2}$				
	16	$.23\ 10^{-2}$	$.23\ 10^{-2}$	$.23\ 10^{-2}$			
	32	$.62\ 10^{-3}$	$.62\ 10^{-3}$	$.62\ 10^{-3}$	$.62\ 10^{-3}$		
	64	$.14\ 10^{-3}$	$.14\ 10^{-3}$	$.14\ 10^{-3}$	$.14\ 10^{-3}$	$.14\ 10^{-3}$	
	128	$.35\ 10^{-4}$	$.34\ 10^{-4}$	$.34\ 10^{-4}$	$.35\ 10^{-4}$	$.35\ 10^{-4}$	$.35\ 10^{-4}$
10	4	$.32\ 10^{0}$					
	8	$.18\ 10^{0}$	$.10\ 10^{0}$				
	16	$.40\ 10^{-1}$	$.12\ 10^{-1}$	$.25\ 10^{-1}$			
	32	$.70\ 10^{-2}$	$.69\ 10^{-2}$	$.60\ 10^{-2}$	$.62\ 10^{-2}$		
	64	$.19\ 10^{-2}$	$.19\ 10^{-2}$	$.19\ 10^{-2}$	$.19\ 10^{-2}$	$.19\ 10^{-2}$	
	128	$.50\ 10^{-3}$	$.50\ 10^{-3}$	$.50\ 10^{-3}$	$.50\ 10^{-3}$	$.50\ 10^{-3}$	$.51\ 10^{-3}$
100	4	$.43\ 10^{+1}$					
	8	$.72\ 10^{+1}$	$.11\ 10^{+1}$				
	16	$.30\ 10^{+2}$	$.11\ 10^{+1}$	$.29\ 10^{0}$			
	32	$.13\ 10^{+4}$	$.13\ 10^{+1}$	$.20\ 10^{0}$	$.10\ 10^{0}$		
	64	$.17\ 10^{+7}$	$.16\ 10^{+1}$	$.41\ 10^{-1}$	$.36\ 10^{-1}$	$.29\ 10^{-1}$	
	128	$.29\ 10^{+13}$	$.26\ 10^{+1}$	$.75\ 10^{-2}$	$.94\ 10^{-2}$	$.10\ 10^{-1}$	$.85\ 10^{-2}$

Table 2.5.3. Reduction factors for the multiple grid method defined by $\tilde{B}_p^{(4)}$.

Using (2.5.2), (2.5.3) and (2.5.6) for the approximation errors we conclude from Theorem 2.4.4 that for the multiple grid methods $\sigma = 2$ iteration steps are sufficient to get an iteration error which is of the same order of magnitude as the approximation errors $\|f-T_p f\|$ and $\|Kf-K_p f\|$. Of course, this is not the case with Atkinson's method for which one has to perform $\mathcal{O}(\log N_p)$ iteration steps. That these asymptotic argument holds already for relatively small N_p is shown in the Tables 2.5.4 - 2.5.5, where we compare the approximation errors with the iteration error after $\sigma = 2$ iteration steps.

λ	N_p	$B_p^{(2)}$	$\tilde{B}_p^{(3)}$	$\tilde{B}_p^{(4)}$
1	4	.0046	.0018	.0018
	8	.0267	.0003	.0003
	16	.1162	.0001	.0001
	32	.4743	.0000	.0000
	64	.0930	.0000	.0000
	128	5.6378	.0000	.0000
10	4	-	3.3089	3.3089
	8	-	-	.0568
	16	-	-	.3899
	32	-	-	.0694
	64	-	-	.0194
	128	-	-	.0050

Table 2.5.4. The ratio: iteration error after 2 sweeps/ approximation errors,

i.e. $\dfrac{\|\tilde{f}_{p,2}-\tilde{f}_{p,\infty}\|}{\|f-\tilde{f}_{p,\infty}\|}$.

Number of subintervals: $N_0 = 2$ (a divergent iteration process is denoted by -).

λ	N_p	$B_p^{(2)}$	$\tilde{B}_p^{(3)}$	$\tilde{B}_p^{(4)}$
1	16	.0003	.0001	.0001
	32	.0017	.0000	.0000
	64	.0075	.0000	.0000
	128	.0306	.0000	.0000
10	16	.0936	.3202	.3202
	32	.6088	.2000	.0692
	64	2.7111	.0341	.0194
	128	11.1310	.0056	.0050
100	16	91.0760	34.0160	34.0160
	32	563.4392	-	34.7089
	64	2480.5082	-	24.3138
	128	$> 10^4$	-	0.1220

Table 2.5.5. The ratio: iteration error after 2 sweeps/ approximation errors.
As Table 2.5.4, but with $N_0 = 8$.

We conclude this section with some remarks about the asymptotic computational complexity. It is our purpose to establish the fast convergence of the multiple grid methods rather than to construct efficient computer codes. Therefore, in our implementation kernel-functions are re-evaluated whenever they are used. Then, the number of kernel evaluations is equal to the number of multiplications involved in the matrix $*$ vector computations defining the operation counts. The overhead costs (a.o. arithmetic operations used for the interaction between the grids) are neglected. Asymptotically for $N_p \to \infty$, the operation counts per iteration for the various approximate inverses are:

$B_p^{(1)}$: $3.25\ N_p^2$, $\quad\tilde{B}_p^{(1)}$: $2.5\ N_p^2$,

$B_p^{(2)}$: $2\ N_p^2$, $\quad\tilde{B}_p^{(2)}$: $2\ N_p^2$,

$B_p^{(3)}$: $2\ N_p^2\ {}^2\log N_p$, $\quad\tilde{B}_p^{(3)}$: $3\ N_p^2$,

$B_p^{(4)}$: $2.5\ N_p^2\ {}^2\log N_p$, $\quad\tilde{B}_p^{(4)}$: $3.5\ N_p^2$.

Here we ignored the direct solution on the coarsest grid and we applied the multiple grid methods with $\gamma = 2$ on all levels.

<u>NOTE</u>. The number of kernel-function evaluations is N_p^2 in the linear case when they are computed once and stored. However, for large values of N_p one may need external devices and the efficiency of the multiple grid algorithms may depend on the I/O-facilities of the computer system. In the nonlinear case or in the case when kernel-functions are re-evaluated whenever they are used, the number of kernel-function evaluations per iteration is equal to the number of multiplications given in the table above.

Asymptotically all methods need only two iterations to obtain a result of the order of the truncation error, except the methods with $B_p^{(2)}$ and $\tilde{B}_p^{(2)}$ which need $\mathcal{O}(\log N_p)$ sweeps. For the methods with $B_p^{(1)}$ and $\tilde{B}_p^{(1)}$ the coarsest grid still has $N_p/2$ mesh-intervals; on this grid the problem is solved by a direct method (e.g. Gauss-elimination) and therefore we have to add $\frac{1}{12} N_p^3$ to the total computational complexity. Thus, for *the total amount of asymptotic computational work* we get the following table:

$$\begin{aligned}
&B_p^{(1)}: \tfrac{1}{12} N_p^3 + 6.5\, N_p^2, && \tilde{B}_p^{(1)}: \tfrac{1}{12} N_p^3 + 5N_p^2,\\
&B_p^{(2)}: \tfrac{2}{3} N_0^3 + \mathcal{O}(N_p^2 \log N_p), && \tilde{B}_p^{(2)}: \tfrac{2}{3} N_0^3 + \mathcal{O}(N_p^2 \log N_p),\\
&B_p^{(3)}: \tfrac{2}{3} N_0^3 + 4N_p^2\, {}^2\!\log N_p, && \tilde{B}_p^{(3)}: \tfrac{2}{3} N_0^3 + 6N_p^2,\\
&B_p^{(4)}: \tfrac{2}{3} N_0^3 + 5N_p^2\, {}^2\!\log N_p, && \tilde{B}_p^{(4)}: \tfrac{2}{3} N_0^3 + 7N_p^2.
\end{aligned}$$

From these tables we see that the multiple grid methods become cheaper than Atkinson's method whenever the latter needs more than three iterations.

In order to get an impression of the qualities of the various methods we suggest to measure by experiments the following ratio (which shows the amount of computational work per digit accuracy obtained):

$$\kappa_\sigma = - \frac{\text{Number of multiplications to obtain } \tilde{f}_{p,\sigma}}{N_p^2 * {}^{10}\!\log \| f - \tilde{f}_{p,\sigma} \|}.$$

For the multiple grid methods we choose $\sigma = 2$ because their reduction factors tend to zero as $N_p \to \infty$. For Atkinson's method we determine σ such that κ_σ is minimal. Better methods are now characterized by a smaller κ_σ.

Table 2.5.6 shows for the multiple grid methods that small values of N_0 are more efficient as long as the process converges. However, within a reasonable range of small N_0, it seems not worthwhile to determine an optimal N_0.

N_0	8	16	32	64
$B_p^{(2)}$	7.55 (11)	3.46 (5)	2.73 (3)	6.20 (2)
$\tilde{B}_p^{(3)}$	-	-8.42 (2)	2.97 (2)	5.95 (2)
$\tilde{B}_p^{(4)}$	2.00 (2)	1.86 (2)	2.20 (2)	6.10 (2)

Table 2.5.6. For problem (2.5.1) with $\lambda = 100$ and $N_p = 128$ the experimental ratios κ_σ, where σ is given between parentheses; for this problem $^{10}\log\| f-\tilde{f}_{p,\infty}\| = -3.5$.

The asymptotic work estimates and the convergence property discussed in Section 2.4 lead us to prefer $\tilde{B}_p^{(3)}$ for $\|K\| \approx 1$ and $\tilde{B}_p^{(4)}$ for $\|K\| \gg 1$. Finally, we remark that the same multiple grid techniques can be applied to nonlinear problems and the structure of multiple grid algorithms yields estimates for the approximation and truncation errors in a natural way. All these features together can be used to construct an automatic program for solving Fredholm integral equations of the second kind. In Chapter 3 such a program is constructed.

REFERENCES TO CHAPTER 2

[1] ANSELONE, P.M., *Collectively compact operator approximation theory*, Englewood Cliffs, New Jersey, Prentice-Hall, 1971.

[2] ATKINSON, K.E., *Iterative variants of the Nyström method for the numerical solution of integral equations*, Numerische Mathematik 22 (1973), pp.17-31.

[3] ATKINSON, K.E., *A survey of numerical methods for the solution of Fredholm integral equations of the second kind*, SIAM, 1976.

[4] BRAKHAGE, H., *Über die numerische Behandlung von Integralgleichungen nach der Quadratur-formelmethode*, Numerische Mathematik 2 (1960), pp.183-196.

[5] BRANDT, A., *Multi-level adaptive solutions to boundary-value problems*, Mathematics of Computation 31 (1977), pp.333-390.

[6] BRANDT, A., *Multi-level adaptive techniques for singular perturbation problems*, in: Numerical Analysis of Singular Perturbation Problems (P.W. Hemker & J.J.H. Miller, eds), Academic Press, London, 1979.

[7] HACKBUSCH, W., *Die schnelle Auflösung der Fredholmschen Integralgleichung zweiter Art*, Beiträge zur Numerischen Mathematik 9 (1981), pp.47-62.

[8] HACKBUSCH, W., *An error analysis of the nonlinear multi-grid method of second kind*, Aplikace Matematiky 26 (1981), pp.18-29.

[9] PRENTER, P.M., *A collocation method for the numerical solution of integral equations*, SIAM J. Numer. Anal. 10 (1973), pp.570-581.

[10] SCHIPPERS, H., *Multi-grid techniques for the solution of Fredholm integral equations of the second kind*, Colloquium Numerical Treatment of Integral Equations, MC-Syllabus 41, Mathematisch Centrum, Amsterdam (1979).

[11] STETTER, H.J., *The defect correction principle and discretization methods*, Numerische Mathematik 29 (1978), pp.425-443.

[12] WESSELING, P. & P. SONNEVELD, *Numerical experiments with a multiple grid and preconditioned Lanczos type method*, Procs of the IUTAM-Symposium on Approximation Methods for Navier-Stokes Problems, 1980, Lecture Notes in Mathematics 771, pp.543-562, Springer.

[13] WESSELING, P., *The rate of convergence of a multiple grid method*, Procs of the Dundee Biennial Conference on Numerical Analysis, 1980, Lecture Notes in Mathematics 773, pp.164-184, Springer.

CHAPTER 3

AUTOMATIC NUMERICAL SOLUTION OF FREDHOLM INTEGRAL EQUATIONS OF THE SECOND KIND

3.1. INTRODUCTION

In this chapter we describe an algorithm for the automatic numerical solution of Fredholm integral equations of the second kind:

$$(3.1.1) \qquad f(x) - \int_a^b k(x,y)f(y)dy = g(x), \qquad x \in [a,b].$$

The algorithm is an improvement of Atkinson's automatic program *iesimp* [3] in the sense that a new iterative method is used for the solution of the system of equations that arises from the approximation of (3.1.1). Our iterative methods are multiple grid methods that work with a sequence of grids of decreasing mesh-size. These grids are used simultaneously to obtain an approximation to the continuous problem (3.1.1). The multiple grid methods used can be seen as extensions of Atkinson's iterative scheme, that uses only two grids: a coarse and a fine grid. Convergence and computational complexity of the multiple grid methods have been studied in Chapter 2. The program has been written in the algorithmic language ALGOL 68, because in this language we can easily and efficiently handle the data structures and the recursive procedures that appear in multiple grid methods.

In Chapter 2 a description of our multiple grid methods has been given by means of collectively compact operators and interpolatory projections onto subspaces of piecewise continuous functions. In Section 3.2 some relevant results are recollected. Based on the theoretical foundation of Section 3.2, the program for the automatic solution of Fredholm equations, *solve int eq*, is described in Section 3.3. Numerical examples illustrating the method are given in Section 3.4, where comparisons are made with Atkinson's automatic program *iesimp*. Further applications of *solve int eq* are described in Chapters 4 and 5.

3.2. THEORETICAL FOUNDATIONS

In this section we write equation (3.1.1) in operator notation as follows:

(3.2.1) $(I-K)f = g, \quad g \in X,$

where X is a Banach space and $K: X \to X$ the linear operator associated with the kernel $k(x,y)$. It is assumed that (I-K) has a bounded inverse on X. We approximate the solution of (3.2.1) by a sequence of interpolating spline functions $\tilde{f}_p$ with knots at the points $G_p = \{t_i \mid a = t_0 < t_1 \ldots < t_{N_p} = b\}$. The grids $\{G_p\}$, $p = 0,1,2,\ldots,\ell$, are constructed such that $G_0 \subset G_1 \subset \ldots \subset G_\ell$. Let h_p be a measure of the mesh-size defined by:

$$h_p = \max_i |t_i - t_{i-1}|.$$

In our algorithm we take the sequence of grids $\{G_p\}$ uniform with $N_p = 2^p N_0$, so that

B1. $h_p = 2^{-p} h_0$.

Let X_p, $p = 0,1,2,\ldots,\ell$ be the finite-dimensional subspaces of interpolating spline functions on G_p and let T_p, $p = 0,1,2,\ldots,\ell$ be the corresponding interpolating operators. With this choice of $\{X_p\}$ and $\{T_p\}$ the Assumptions A1 - A2 of Section 2.2 are satisfied. As in Section 2.2 we approximate K by a sequence of approximating operators $\{K_p\}$, $K_p: X \to X$, satisfying the Assumptions A3 - A5 of Section 2.2. Moreover, we make some assumptions about the smoothing properties of $\{K_p\}$ and the order of approximation of the operators $\{K_p\}$ and $\{T_p\}$. Let S be the following subset of X:

$$S = \{K_p f \mid p \geq 0 \text{ and } \|f\| \leq 1\}.$$

By Assumption A4 this set has compact closure in X. In this chapter we take the stronger assumption that the functions in S are sufficiently smooth. Furthermore, for $p \to \infty$ we assume:

B2. $\sup_{f \in S} \|(K-K_p)f\| \leq C_1 h_p^\alpha, \quad \alpha > 0,$

B3. $\sup_{f \in S} \|(I-T_p)f\| \leq C_2 h_p^\beta, \quad \beta > 0.$

The constants α and β are associated with the order of the integration rule (e.g. trapezoidal rule) and of the interpolating spline function. These assumptions are illustrated by the following examples. Let X be the Banach space C[a,b] of continuous functions, provided with the supremum norm. Assume that the kernel function $k(x,y)$ is twice continuous differentiable with respect to x. For this class of kernel functions the Assumptions B2 and B3 can be verified for the following example.

EXAMPLE 1. The operator K_p is defined by the repeated trapezoidal rule and the operator T_p by continuous, piecewise linear interpolation. In this case $\alpha = \beta = 2$.

Analogously we obtain the following example if $k(x,y)$ is four times continuously differentiable with respect to x.

EXAMPLE 2. K_p is defined by the repeated Simpson rule and T_p by continuous, piecewise cubic interpolation. In this case $\alpha = \beta = 4$.

EXAMPLE 3. *Finite element methods for integral equations from potential theory.* Let D be a simply connected finite plane region bounded by a smooth contour S with continuous curvature. S is given by the parametric equations $x = X(s)$, $y = Y(s)$, $s \in [0,1]$. The kernel function is given by

$$k(s,t) = -\frac{1}{\pi}\frac{d}{dt}\arctan\left(\frac{Y(t)-Y(s)}{X(t)-X(s)}\right).$$

For the interpolating spline functions we take the piecewise constant functions (i.e. step-functions). The space X must be chosen such that for each N it contains this class of functions. Furthermore, pointwise operations should be defined on X. Therefore we choose X to be the Banach space of regulated functions (see Section 4.2), provided with the essential supremum norm. The operator T_p is defined by piecewise constant interpolation at the midpoints. For this particular example it is not necessary to approximate the integral operator because $T_pK\tilde{f}_p$ ($\tilde{f}_p \in X_p$) can be computed analytically. However, the theoretical results of Chapter 2 apply if K_p is defined by KT_p. From the results given in Chapter 4 it follows that $\alpha = 1+\rho$, where ρ is a measure for the smoothness of S ($0 < \rho < 1$) and $\beta = 1$.

For these examples we obtain the following estimates for a_p and b_p, which were defined in Lemma 2.2.2 and 2.2.5, respectively.

Example 1: $a_p = O(h_p^2)$, $b_p = O(h_p^2)$.

Example 2: $a_p = O(h_p^4)$, $b_p = O(h_p^4)$.

Example 3: $a_p = O(h_p^{1+\rho})$, $b_p = O(h_p)$.

On level p we wish to approximate the solution of equation (3.2.1) by:

$$(3.2.2) \qquad \tilde{A}_p \tilde{f}_p = T_p g, \quad \tilde{f}_p \in X_p,$$

where $\tilde{A}_p = I - T_p K_p$. We assume that the mesh-size h_0 is sufficiently small such that $\tilde{A}_p^{-1}$ exists for all $p \geq 0$. If the forcing-function g(x) is sufficiently differentiable such that $\|(K-K_p)g\| \leq C_3 h_p^{\alpha}$, it follows from Assumption B2 that $\|(K-K_p)f\| \leq C_4 h_p^{\alpha}$. From Lemma 2.2.6 we deduce:

$$(3.2.3) \qquad \|T_p f - \tilde{f}_p\| \leq C_5 \|(K-K_p)f\| \leq C_4 C_5 h_p^{\alpha} \quad \text{for } p \to \infty.$$

In *solve int eq* we use this asymptotic behaviour of the error to extrapolate and predict the size of the error for small values of h_p.

The solution $\tilde{f}_p \in X_p$ of (3.2.2) is approximated by the defect correction process given by (2.4.2). We notice that the approximate inverse $\tilde{B}_p^{(1)}$ is only of theoretical value, since the dimension of the matrix corresponding to $\tilde{A}_{p-1} T_{p-1}$ tends to infinity as $p \to \infty$. Furthermore, in Section 2.5 it has been demonstrated that $\tilde{B}_p^{(4)}$ yields a multiple grid method with better convergence properties than $\tilde{B}_p^{(3)}$ if the integral operator has a large value for $\|K\|$. Therefore, in our code we apply the approximate inverse $\tilde{B}_p^{(4)}$ rather than $\tilde{B}_p^{(3)}$. Defining the reduction factor $\eta_p^{(j)}$ as in Section 2.4, we obtain:

<u>THEOREM</u> 3.2.1.
(i) $\eta_p^{(1)} \leq C_6 h_p^{\min(\alpha,\beta)}$;
(ii) $\eta_p^{(4)} \leq \eta_p^{(1)} + \eta_p^{(4)^{\gamma}} [\eta_p^{(1)} + \|T_p\|]$.

<u>PROOF</u>. See Theorems 2.4.1 and 2.4.2. □

Based on part (i) of this theorem, the Defect Correction Process induced by $\tilde{B}_p^{(1)}$ can be expected to have a geometric reduction factor, i.e.

$$\|\tilde{f}_{p,i+1} - \tilde{f}_p\| / \|\tilde{f}_{p,i} - \tilde{f}_p\| \to v_p, \quad \text{as } i \to \infty.$$

By Assumption B1 it follows that $v_p = v_1 d^{p-1}$ with $d = 2^{-\min(\alpha,\beta)}$.

The multiple grid process is constructed in such a way that $\tilde{B}_1^{(1)} = \tilde{B}_1^{(4)}$. As a consequence the reduction factor of the multiple grid process depends on the magnitude of v_1, γ and $\|T_p\|$. This dependence is analysed by means of the sequence $\{w_p\}$ defined by:

$$(3.2.4)\qquad \begin{cases} w_1 = v_1, \quad v_p = v_1 d^{p-1}, \\ w_p = v_p + w_{p-1}^{\gamma}(v_p + C), \qquad p > 1, \end{cases}$$

where $C = \sup_{p\geq 0} \|T_p\|$. From Theorem 2.4.3 it follows that $\eta_p^{(4)} \leq 2v_p$ if

$$(3.2.5)\qquad v_1 < \tfrac{1}{2}\left\{\sqrt{1 + (\tfrac{C}{d})^2} - \tfrac{C}{d}\right\}.$$

For d = 1/4 the multiple grid convergence region has been given in Figure 2.1. For other values of d the required upper bounds are given in Table 3.2.1.

d \ C	1	6	24
1/16	1.56(-2)	2.60(-3)	6.51(-4)
1/4	6.16(-2)	1.04(-2)	2.60(-3)
1/2	1.18(-1)	2.08(-2)	5.21(-3)

Table 3.2.1. Upper bounds on v_1 to obtain $w_p \leq 2v_p$, with $\gamma = 2$.

On the coarsest grid the system of equations is solved by Gaussian-elimination. The available storage space of the computer yields an upper bound for N_0 (the number of mesh-intervals of the coarsest grid). The upper bounds on v_1 are essentially the requirement of "a fine enough mesh" in the coarsest discretization of the multiple grid algorithm, i.e. condition (3.2.5) yields a lower bound for N_0. In practice, (3.2.5) is not usable because the required number of mesh-intervals of the coarsest grid (N_0) often exceeds the upper bound. Therefore, in *solve int eq* (3.2.5) is replaced by the weaker condition that two multiple grid iterations must have the same reduction factor as one application of (2.4.2) with approximate inverse $\tilde{B}_p^{(1)}$:

$$(3.2.6)\qquad w_p^2 \leq v_p, \quad p = 1,2,\ldots,\ell.$$

In Table 3.2.2 we give the resulting upper bounds on v_1, which have been obtained numerically as follows. Define the function

$$F(v_1) \equiv w_\ell^2 - v_\ell,$$

with ℓ sufficiently large, and solve $F(v_1) = 0$ by means of bisection.

d \ C	1	6	24
1/16	3.51 - 1	9.11 - 2	2.81 - 2
1/4	4.47 - 1	1.17 - 1	3.27 - 2
1/2	4.34 - 1	1.10 - 1	2.93 - 2

Table 3.2.2. Upper bounds on v_1 to obtain $w_p^2 \leq v_p$, with $\gamma = 2$.

Comparing Tables 3.2.1 and 3.2.2 we conclude that (3.2.6) yields larger values for the upper bounds on v_1 than (3.2.5). Hence, Condition (3.2.6) requires a smaller number of mesh-intervals on the coarsest grid, so that a more robust algorithm is obtained. Without danger of confusion we further use η_p for $\eta_p^{(4)}$.

In *solve int eq* we start on some coarse grid and we estimate v_1. A test is made to check whether (3.2.6) is satisfied. The constant w_p ($p > 1$) follows from (3.2.4) as soon as v_1 has been determined. Since $\eta_p \leq w_p$ it follows that

$$(3.2.7) \qquad \|\tilde{f}_{p,i+1} - \tilde{f}_p\| \leq w_p \|\tilde{f}_{p,i} - \tilde{f}_p\|.$$

After σ iterations the multiple grid process yields an approximate solution $\tilde{f}_{p,\sigma}$ for which the following error estimate holds:

$$(3.2.8) \qquad \|T_p f - \tilde{f}_{p,\sigma}\| \leq \|T_p f - \tilde{f}_p\| + \|\tilde{f}_{p,\sigma} - \tilde{f}_p\|.$$

In our code *solve int eq* we determine the integers p and σ in an automatic way such that $\|T_p f - \tilde{f}_{p,\sigma}\|$ is less than a prescribed value *tol*. This is achieved by estimating the errors on the right-hand side of (3.2.8). Asymptotically for $p \to \infty$, Condition (3.2.6) ensures that only two multiple grid iterations yield a result of the order of the approximation error $\| T_p f - \tilde{f}_p \|$. On the lower levels (i.e. small p) we determine σ such that

$$(3.2.9) \qquad \| \tilde{f}_{p,\sigma} - \tilde{f}_p \| \le 0.1 * \| T_p f - \tilde{f}_p \| ,$$

i.e. the iteration error must be less than the approximation error.

3.3. AUTOMATIC PROGRAM

In this section we describe our code *solve int eq*, a program for the automatic solution of the Fredholm equation (3.1.1). Like Atkinson's program *iesimp* the procedure is divided into two stages. In stage A we determine the coarsest mesh-width h_0 by means of (2.4.2) with the approximate inverse $\tilde{B}_1^{(1)}$. The reduction factor v_1 is estimated by

$$v_1 = \max_{i=0,1,\ldots,5} \| \tilde{f}_{1,i+2} - \tilde{f}_{1,i+1} \| / \| \tilde{f}_{1,i+1} - \tilde{f}_{1,i} \| ,$$

with $\tilde{f}_{1,0} = T_1 \tilde{f}_0$.

If the reduction factor v_1 appears sufficiently small such that $w_p^2 < v_p$, then stage B is entered. Otherwise, the number of points N_0 is doubled. In stage B the number of levels is increased until the predicted error estimate for $\| T_p f - \tilde{f}_{p,\sigma} \|$ is less than *tol*. The reduction factor of the multiple grid process is estimated by w_p (3.2.4) and the previously determined value of v_1. Using (3.2.7) we estimate the iteration error by

$$(3.3.1) \qquad \| \tilde{f}_{p,\sigma} - \tilde{f}_p \| \le w_p / (1 - w_p) \| \tilde{f}_{p,\sigma} - \tilde{f}_{p,\sigma-1} \| .$$

As the number of levels increases we are able to estimate the ratio

$$r = \| T_p f - \tilde{f}_p \| / \| T_{p-1} f - \tilde{f}_{p-1} \| .$$

Asymptotically for $p \to \infty$, this ratio approximates the value $2^{-\alpha}$; see Assumption B1 and (3.2.3). In this chapter we only apply multiple grid methods to approximating operators K_p with $\alpha > 1$. Hence, the ratio r must be less than 0.5. Initially we set $r = 0.5$ and we compute the above ratio by

$$r = \min\left(0.5, \max\left(2^{-\alpha}, \frac{\| T_{p-1}\tilde{f}_p - \tilde{f}_{p-1}\|}{\| T_{p-2}\tilde{f}_{p-1} - \tilde{f}_{p-2}\|}\right)\right).$$

Using this value of r we estimate the approximation error by:

$$\text{(3.3.2)} \qquad \| T_p f - \tilde{f}_p \| \le r/(1-r) \| T_{p-1}\tilde{f}_{p,\sigma} - \tilde{f}_{p-1} \| .$$

The error estimates (3.3.1) and (3.3.2) are used to verify the test (3.2.9). If it is satisfied, then we set $\tilde{f}_p := \tilde{f}_{p,\sigma}$. Otherwise, a new iterate is computed and test (3.2.9) is repeated. If the error estimate (3.3.2) yields a value less than *tol*, then the computations are terminated and *solve int eq* returns successfully.

Asymptotically for $p \to \infty$, the total amount of work on level p can be computed. For the Examples 1 and 2 the operation counts per iteration for $\tilde{B}_p^{(4)}$ (with $\gamma = 2$) are $3.5\ N_p^2$. Condition (3.2.6) ensures that only two iterates need to be calculated. The first iterate is obtained by interpolating the results of level p-1. Therefore the total amount of work is equal to:

$$\text{(3.3.3)} \qquad (1 + \tfrac{1}{4} + \tfrac{1}{16} + \ldots)\ 3.5\ N_p^2 = 4\tfrac{2}{3}\ N_p^2 .$$

For the description of our code *solve int eq* we use the programming language ALGOL 68 [5], because this language can easily handle the data structures and the recursive procedures that appear in multiple grid algorithms.

In order to present our program in a concise, modular and easily readable form, we first give an informal description of a set of ALGOL 68 modes and operators that correspond to the mathematical objects and operators of Section 3.2. The formal description of the modes and operators is their ALGOL 68 implementation which we give in the Appendix to this chapter (p. 54).

```
MODE VEC          = REF [ ] REAL:
                      # a structure to represent an element of Xp,
                        i.e. the nodal values of the spline representation #.
MODE MAT          = REF [,] REAL:
                      # a structure to represent a matrix #.
```

PROC restrict	:=	*(VEC y_p) VEC*: # a representation of the operator T_{p-1} mapping X_p onto X_{p-1}, *restrict (y_p)* delivers $T_{p-1}\, y_p$ #.
PROC prolongate	:=	*(VEC y_p) VEC*: # a representation of the operator T_{p+1} mapping X_p onto X_{p+1}, *prolongate (y_p)* delivers $T_{p+1}\, y_p$ #.
PROC project	:=	*(INT p, PROC (REAL) REAL f) VEC*: # a representation of the operator T_p mapping X onto X_p, *project (p,f)* delivers $T_p f$ #.
INT n0	=	# an integer to represent the dimension of X_0 #.
PROC n	=	*(INT p) INT: n0*2**p;* # delivers the value N_p #.
PROC level	=	*(INT n_p) INT*: # level number as follows from n_p and *n0* #.
PROC zero	=	*(INT p) VEC*: # delivers the zero-element of X_p #.
PROC q	:=	*(INT ℓ, VEC y_p) VEC*: # a representation of the operator K_p mapping X_p onto X_ℓ, *q(ℓ,y_p)* delivers $T_\ell K_p y_p$ #.
PROC solve directly	=	*(MAT a, VEC f,g) VOID*: # solve directly determines the solution of $af = g$ by means of Gaussian-elimination) #.
PROC evaluate jacobian	=	*(INT p, VEC y_p) MAT*: # evaluates the matrix $T_p(I-K_p)$ #.
PROC norm	=	*(VEC y_p) REAL*: # delivers the ℓ_∞-norm of y_p #.
PROC kk	:=	*(REAL x,y,fy) REAL:* # a representation of the integrand of (3.1.1), *kk(x,y,fy)* = k(x,y)*f(y) #.
PROC forcey	:=	*(REAL x) REAL:* # a representation of the right-hand side of (3.1.1) #.

TEXT 3.3.1. An informal description of modes, operators and procedures used in *solve int eq*.

The implementation in an ALGOL 68 program of these operators and procedures depends on the choice of $\{G_p\}$, the approximating operators $\{K_p\}$ and the interpolation operators $\{T_p\}$. An implementation of Example 1 and 2 of

Section 3.2 is given in the Appendix (p. 54).

The approximating inverse $\tilde{B}_p^{(4)}$ is defined recursively and depends on a positive integer γ (fixed for all p). However, a more robust algorithm is obtained if γ can be adapted to the level number p. Therefore, in our implementation of the multiple grid algorithm γ depends on p (i.e. in the definition of $\tilde{Q}_p^{(4)}$ we replace γ by γ_p). Inside *solve int eq* a procedure, called *examine convergence*, is specified which determines γ_p, $p = 1,2,\ldots,\ell-1$, (ℓ is the highest level which follows from N_ℓ and N_0). This procedure is of a heuristic structure. In its most simple form it would set $\gamma_p = 2$, for all p. Depending on the behaviour of the actual, iterative process it would adapt γ_p. In order to retain our computational complexity of $O(N^2)$ we take care that $\gamma_p \leq 3$. An exception is made for the lowest level (γ_1 may increase to 5). The multiple grid method obtained in this way is given in Text 3.3.2.

```
PROC mulgrid = ( INT m,sigma,[] INT gamma, MAT jacobian,
                  REF VEC um, VEC rhsm, BOOL um is zero) VOID :
IF   m = 0
THEN solve directly(jacobian,um,rhsm)
ELSE BOOL uz:= um is zero;
     FOR it TO sigma
     DO VEC rm    = ( uz ! rhsm ! rhsm-um+q(m,um));
        VEC umm1:= zero(m-1);
        VEC rmm1 = restrict(rm);
        VEC fmm1 = rmm1-q(m-1,rmm1)+q(m-1,rm);
        mulgrid(m-1,gamma[m],gamma,jacobian,umm1,fmm1, TRUE );
        um:= um + rm + prolongate(umm1-rmm1);
        uz:= FALSE
     OD
FI    ;
```

<u>TEXT 3.3.2.</u> Implementation of the multiple grid method defined by (2.4.2) and $\tilde{B}_p^{(4)}$.

The procedure *solve int eq* for the automatic solution of Fredholm equations of the second kind is described in Text 3.3.3. The user has to specify upper limits for N_0 and N_ℓ, i.e. the maximum number of intervals in the coarsest and the finest discretization. Furthermore, *solve int eq* needs information about α (see Assumption B3) and $\|T_p\|$ (see (3.2.4)).

```
PROC solve int eq = ( REF INT n0, INT n0upper,nlupper, REAL tol,
                      alfa,normt, REF VEC um, REF REAL error)  BOOL :
BEGIN

  PROC determine v1 = ( REF REAL numv1,denv1,v1, REF VEC um,
                        VEC rhs) VOID :
  ( VEC umold:= COPY um;
    mulgrid  (1,1,gamma,jacobian,um,rhs, FALSE );
    numv1:= norm(um-umold); REAL v1old:= 0.0;
    FOR  it TO 5
    WHILE umold:= COPY um;
          mulgrid (1,1,gamma,jacobian,um,rhs, FALSE );
          denv1:= numv1; numv1:= norm(umold-um);
          IF  numv1 > min((tol,1.0e-12))
          THEN (it > 1 ! v1old:= v1 );
                v1:= numv1/denv1;
                it<3 OR ABS (v1-v1old) > 0.02*v1old
          ELSE ( it=1 ! v1*:= ratio ); v1old:=v1; FALSE
          FI
    DO   SKIP   OD ;
    v1:= 1.02*max((v1old,v1))                    );

  PROC examine convergence = ( REAL v1, INT levels, REF [] INT gamma)
        BOOL :
  ( gamma[1]:= 0; BOOL conv;
    FOR  ii TO levels+2
    WHILE IF   ii <= levels
          THEN FOR i FROM 2 TO ii DO gamma[i]:= 3 OD
          ELIF ii=levels+1 THEN gamma[2]:= 4
          ELIF ii=levels+2 THEN gamma[2]:= 5
          FI   ;
          REAL vp:= v1,wp:= v1;
          IF   conv:= ( wp*wp <= vp )
          THEN FOR    p FROM 2 TO levels
               WHILE vp *:= ratio;
                     wp  := vp+wp**gamma[p]*(vp+normt);
                     conv:= ( wp*wp <= vp )
               DO    SKIP    OD
          FI ;
          ( NOT conv) AND n0 = n0upper
    DO   SKIP  OD ;
    print(newline);
    FOR ii TO levels DO print((whole(gamma[ii],4))) OD ;
    conv          );

  PROC v1 on level = ( INT m) REAL :
  ( REAL vp:= v1, wp:= v1;
    FOR p FROM 2 TO m
    DO vp:= ratio*vp; wp:= vp+wp**gamma[p]*(vp+normt) OD ;
    wp       );

  INT  levels:= level(nlupper); HEAP [1:levels] INT gamma;
  FOR  j TO levels DO gamma[j]:= 2 OD ;
  REAL ratio = 0.5**alfa;
  REAL v1:=1.0,denv1,numv1,v2:=0.5,denv2,numv2:=1.0; error:= maxreal;
  BOOL rapidconvergence;
  VEC  rhs, umm1; MAT jacobian;
```

```
#******************      stage a     ********************************#

  FOR  loop
  WHILE um:= zero(0); rhs:=project(0,forcey);
        jacobian:= evaluate jacobian(0,um);
        solve directly(jacobian,um,rhs);
        IF   loop>1
        THEN denv2:=numv2; numv2:=norm(restrict(um)-umm1);
             (loop>2 ! v2:= max((ratio,min((0.5,numv2/denv2)))) );
             error:=(v2/(1-v2))*numv2
        FI ;
        IF   error>tol
        THEN rhs  := project(1,forcey);
             umm1 := COPY um;
             um   := prolongate(umm1);
             determine v1(numv1,denv1,v1,um,rhs);
             rapidconvergence:= examine convergence(v1,levels,gamma)
        FI ;
        error>tol AND ( NOT rapidconvergence) AND n0upper >= 2*n0
  DO   n0*:= 2; levels-:= 1 OD  ;

#****************** end of stage a    ******************************#

  IF   NOT rapidconvergence
  THEN print((newline," multigrid convergence too slow "))
  FI   ;

#******************       stage b     ********************************#

  IF   error > tol AND rapidconvergence
  THEN FOR  m TO levels
       WHILE denv2:=numv2;  numv2:= norm(restrict(um)-umm1);
             REAL rt   := min((ratio,v2));
             REAL wm    = v1 on level(m);
             REAL v1m  := wm;
             FOR  imax TO 5
             WHILE numv1 > 0.1*((1.0-v1m)/v1m)*(rt/(1.0-rt))*numv2
                    # extra iteration: #
             DO   denv1:= numv1;
                  VEC umold:= COPY um;
                  mulgrid (m,1,gamma,jacobian,um,rhs, FALSE );
                  numv1:= norm(um-umold);
                  numv2:= norm(restrict(um)-umm1);
                  v1m  := min((wm,numv1/denv1))
             OD   ;
             v2   := max((ratio,min((0.5,numv2/denv2))));
             error:= (v2/(1-v2))*numv2;
             error>tol AND m<levels
       DO   rhs := project(m+1,forcey);
            umm1:= COPY um; um:= prolongate(umm1);
            VEC umold:= COPY um;
            mulgrid (m+1,1,gamma,jacobian,um,rhs, FALSE );
            numv1:= norm(um-umold)
       OD
  FI   ;

#****************** end of stage b    ******************************#
```

```
  error <= tol OR rapidconvergence
END # solve int eq #   ;
```

TEXT 3.3.3. Implementation of *solve int eq*.

We could use a slight modification of the above program to implement Atkinson's [3] FORTRAN code *iesimp* in ALGOL 68. Because of the modular structure of *solve int eq* it is also easy to program other numerical methods for integral equations (e.g. higher order formules for smooth kernel functions). Furthermore, *solve int eq* can be applied to multi-dimensional integral equations (e.g. potential flow around three-dimensional bodies [6]) and non-linear integral equations, such as the equations describing the oscillating disk flow studied in Chapter 5.

3.4. NUMERICAL RESULTS

In this section we illustrate Examples 1 - 2 of Section 3.2 for a variety of problems. The problems contain parameters λ,ρ,μ, which have been chosen such that $\|(I-T_pK_p)^{-1}\|$ is large. This means that large linear systems are necessary to obtain a reasonably accurate approximation $\tilde{f}_p(x)$ ($\tilde{f}_p \in X_p$) to the exact solution $f(x)$.

For the Problems 1 - 3 (taken from ATKINSON [3]) we give the performances of both *solve int eq* and Atkinson's program *iesimp*. In the tables we give the final number of intervals on the lowest and on the highest level (N_0 and N_ℓ, respectively) and the number of work units (WU), where 1 WU is defined by N_ℓ^2 kernel evaluations.

NOTE. For Examples 1 and 2 of Section 3.2 the number of kernel evaluations is N_ℓ^2, when the values are computed once and stored (Example 3 $\approx \frac{4}{3} N_\ell^2$). However, when they are not stored the number of kernel evaluations is a good measure for the computational complexity of the algorithms *solve int eq* and *iesimp*.

Case (i):

$$k(x,y) = \begin{cases} -\lambda x(1-y), & 0 \le x \le y \le 1, \\ -\lambda y(1-x), & 0 \le y \le x \le 1. \end{cases}$$

Since this kernel function is not continuously differentiable for $x = y$, we define K_p by the repeated trapezoidal rule. Assumption B3 is satisfied with

$\alpha = 2$. The interpolatory spline functions are defined by linear interpolation. The right-hand side $g(x)$ is chosen such that the solution of (3.1.1) is $f(x) = \mu^2 x^\mu (1-x)$, $\mu \geq 1$.

NOTE. In [3] ATKINSON solves this problem by Simpson's rule, but he remarks that the order of convergence is $\mathcal{O}(h^2)$. Therefore, in Table 3.4.1 the numerical results of *iesimp* (which are obtained by Simpson's rule) can be compared with the results of *solve int eq*.

	λ	Error		Final		
		Predicted	Actual	N_0	N_ℓ	WU
solve i.	-10.0	8.48 (-4)	7.35 (-4)	32	256	4.83 (1)
iesimp	-10.0	8.93 (-4)	1.03 (-3)	16	256	9.23
solve i.	-30.0	5.52 (-4)	5.48 (-4)	16	128	5.61
iesimp	-30.0	8.91 (-4)	8.93 (-4)	8	128	6.76
solve i.	-90.0	4.85 (-3)	3.86 (-3)	32	256	10.65 (2)
iesimp	-90.0	7.71 (-3)	5.96 (-3)	32	256	13.60 (2)
solve i.	90.0	3.01 (-4)	2.93 (-4)	16	128	8.15 (3)
iesimp	90.0	3.78 (-4)	2.18 (-4)	32	256	8.06 (3)

Table 3.4.1. Results for case (i), $\mu = 5$.
For *iesimp* K_p is defined by Simpson's rule, for *solve int eq* by the trapezoidal rule.
Tolerance (*tol*) = 1.0 (-3).

NOTES to Table 3.4.1.

Note (1): For this problem *solve int eq* needs 4.83 WU, which is already close to the asymptotic value of 4 2/3 WU (see Equation (3.3.3)).

Note (2): For the tolerance specified both *iesimp* and *solve int eq* cannot solve this problem with 256 intervals on the highest level. In this case we took *nℓupper* = 256 and therefore both codes fail.

Note (3): For this problem *iesimp* needs 256 intervals, whereas *solve int eq* returns successfully with 128 intervals on the highest level. Hence, for this case the cost of *solve int eq* is about 25% of the cost of *iesimp* (note the definition of WU).

Case (ii): $k(x,y) = \lambda \cos(\mu^2 \pi xy)$, $0 \le x, y \le 1$.

The oscillatory behaviour of this kernel function increases as μ increases. The value of λ is chosen close to characteristic values; see ATKINSON [3]. Since $k(x,y)$ is several times continuously differentiable we use Simpson's rule and cubic interpolation to define K_p and T_p, respectively (i.e. Example 2 of Section 3.2 with $\alpha = \beta = 4$ and $\|T_p\| = 24$).

The right-hand side is chosen such that $f(x) = e^{\mu x} \cos(7\mu x)$.

	λ	μ	Error		Final		
			Predicted	Actual	N_0	N_ℓ	WU
solve i.	-2000	1.0	8.41 (-6)	8.37 (-6)	32	256	6.00 (1)
iesimp	-2000	1.0	9.75 (-6)	8.68 (-6)	32	256	7.83
solve i.	-1.42	2.0	3.57 (-6)	3.56 (-6)	16	256	4.17
iesimp	-1.42	2.0	3.58 (-6)	3.57 (-6)	16	256	6.60

Table 3.4.2. Results for case (ii).
The operator K_p is defined by Simpson's rule.
Tolerance (*tol*) = 1.0 (-5).

Note (1): For this case *solve int eq* did not use the default values of γ_p, ($p = 1,2$), but on level 1 the value of γ_p was adapted (i.e. $\gamma_1 = 3$, $\gamma_2 = 2$).

Case (iii): $k(x,y) = \mu/[\mu^2+(x-y)^2]$, $\mu > 0$, $0 \le x, y \le 1$.

This kernel is increasingly peaked as $\mu \to 0$. For $\mu = 0.1$ the ratio $k_{max}/k_{min} = 101$.

We determine the right-hand side such that $f(x) = x^2 - 0.8x + 0.06$. For the definition of K_p and T_p we refer to Example 2 of Section 3.2. The numerical results are given in Table 3.4.3.

	λ	Error Tolerance	Predicted	Actual	Final N_0	N_ℓ	WU
solve i.	0.52	1.0 (-7)	3.42 (-8)	3.40 (-8)	32	256	4.83
iesimp	0.52	1.0 (-7)	3.43 (-8)	3.41 (-8)	32	256	7.83
solve i.	0.95	1.0 (-6)	1.55 (-7)	1.54 (-7)	32	256	5.22
iesimp	0.95	1.0 (-6)	1.56 (-7)	1.55 (-7)	32	256	7.83
solve i.	10.0	1.0 (-6)	1.65 (-7)	1.59 (-7)	32	256	8.14 (1)
iesimp	10.0	1.0 (-6)	2.90 (-7)	2.70 (-7)	32	256	7.83

Table 3.4.3. Results for case (iii), $\mu = 0.1$.
The operator K_p is defined by Simpson's rule.

Note (1): In this problem *solve int eq* adapted the values of γ to $\gamma_1 = 5$ and $\gamma_2 = 3$. Moreover, an additional iteration was performed on the highest level because test (3.2.9) was not satisfied after one iteration. Therefore, the computational work deviates from the asymptotic amount given by (3.3.3).

From the Tables 3.4.1 - 3.4.3 we conclude that Atkinson's code *iesimp* is on the average about 50% more expensive than *solve int eq*. In all experiments both procedures very accurately predict the error of the obtained solution.

Case (iv): For Example 3 of Section 3.2 our code *solve int eq* is applied to the calculation of non-circulatory, potential flow around a smooth contour. The numerical results are presented in Section 4.4.

The numerical results of this section were computed on a CDC-CYBER 175 in single precision arithmetic.

REFERENCES TO CHAPTER 3

[1] ANSELONE, P.M., *Collectively compact operator approximation theory*, Englewood Cliffs, New Jersey, Prentice-Hall, 1971.

[2] ATKINSON, K.E., *A survey of numerical methods for the solution of Fredholm integral equations of the second kind*, SIAM, 1976.

[3] ATKINSON, K.E., *An automatic program for linear Fredholm integral equations of the second kind*, ACM Transactions on Mathematical Software 2 (1976), pp.154-171.

[4] PRENTER, P.M., *A collocation method for the numerical solution of integral equations*, SIAM J. Numer. Anal. 10 (1973), pp.570-581.

[5] VAN WIJNGAARDEN et al., Eds (1976), *Revised Report on the Algorithmic Language ALGOL 68*, Springer-Verlag, New York, Heidelberg, Berlin (1976).

[6] WOLFF, H., *Multigrid method for the calculation of potential flow around 3-D bodies*, Report NW 119, Mathematisch Centrum, Amsterdam, 1982.

APPENDIX TO CHAPTER 3

```
BEGIN # automatic solution of fredholm equations of the second kind #

   MODE INTERVAL = STRUCT ( REAL begin,end);
   MODE VEC = REF [ ] REAL ;
   MODE MAT = REF [,] REAL ;

   OP ** = ( REAL x,y) REAL : ( x <= 0.0 ! 0.0 ! exp(y*ln(x)) );

   OP + = ( VEC a,b) VEC :
   ( INT l= LWB a, u= UPB a; VEC c = HEAP [l:u] REAL ;
     FOR i FROM l TO u DO c[i]:= a[i] + b[i] OD ;
     c ) # vec + vec #;

   OP - = ( VEC a,b) VEC :
   ( INT l= LWB a, u= UPB a; VEC c = HEAP [l:u] REAL ;
     FOR i FROM l TO u DO c[i]:= a[i] - b[i] OD ;
     c ) # vec - vec #;

   OP / = ( VEC a, REAL b) VEC :
   ( INT l= LWB a, u= UPB a; VEC c = HEAP [l:u] REAL ;
     FOR i FROM l TO u DO c[i]:= a[i] / b  OD ;
     c ) # vec / real #;

   OP * = ( REAL b, VEC a) VEC :
   ( INT l= LWB a, u= UPB a; VEC c = HEAP [l:u] REAL ;
     FOR i FROM l TO u DO c[i]:= b * a[i] OD ;
     c ) # real * vec #;

   OP * = ( VEC a, b) REAL :
   ( INT l= LWB a, u= UPB a; REAL c:= 0.0;
     FOR i FROM l TO u DO c +:= a[i]*b[i] OD ;
     c ) # vec * vec #;

   OP * = ( MAT a, VEC b) VEC :
   ( INT l=1 LWB a, u=1 UPB a; VEC c = HEAP [l:u] REAL ;
     FOR i FROM l TO u DO c[i] := a[i, ]*b[ ] OD ;
     c ) # mat * vec #;

   OP COPY = ( VEC u) VEC :
   ( INT l = LWB u, up = UPB u; VEC c = HEAP [l:up] REAL ;
     FOR i FROM l TO up DO c[i]:= u[i] OD ;
     c  )  ;

   PROC prvec = ( VEC x) VOID :
   ( print((" vec bounds ", LWB x, UPB x,newline));
     FOR i FROM LWB x TO UPB x
     DO  print(x[i]) OD ;
     print(newline) );
```

```
PROC max = ([] REAL a ) REAL :
( INT l= LWB a, u= UPB a; REAL s:=a[l];
  FOR i FROM l+1 TO u DO ( a[i]>s ! s:=a[i] ) OD ;
  s );

PROC min = ([] REAL a ) REAL :
( INT l= LWB a, u= UPB a; REAL s:=a[l];
  FOR i FROM l+1 TO u DO ( a[i]<s ! s:=a[i] ) OD ;
  s );

PROC norm = ( VEC a) REAL :
( INT l= LWB a, u= UPB a; REAL s:= ABS a[l];
  FOR i FROM l+1 TO u
  DO REAL b = ABS a[i]; ( b>s ! s:=b ) OD ;
  s );

PROC n = ( INT l) INT :( n0 * 2**l );

PROC level = ( INT nb) INT :
( INT  s:= n(0), l:= 0;
  WHILE s < nb DO l+:= 1; s:= 2*s OD ;
  IF   s > nb THEN error FI ; l );

PROC zero = ( INT l) VEC :
( INT nl = n(l); VEC bb = HEAP [0:nl] REAL ;
  FOR i FROM 0 TO nl DO bb[i]:= 0.0 OD ;bb);

PROC pinject = ( INT l, PROC ( REAL ) REAL f) VEC :
( INT nl= n(l);              HEAP [0:nl] REAL yl;
  REAL a:= begin OF int; REAL h = (end OF int - a)/nl;
  yl[0]:= f(a);
  FOR i TO nl
  DO yl[i]:= f( a+:=h ) OD ; yl );

PROC inject = ( VEC vp) VEC :
( INT np = UPB vp, nq = np OVER 2;
  VEC vq = HEAP [0:nq] REAL ;
  FOR i FROM 0 TO nq DO vq[i]:= vp[2*i] OD ; vq);

#******************     example 1     ********************************#

PROC lin int = ( VEC vp) VEC :
( INT np = UPB vp; INT nq = 2*np;
  VEC vq = HEAP [0:nq] REAL ;
  vq[0]:= vp[0];
  FOR i TO np
  DO  vq[2*i]   := vp[i];
      vq[2*i-1]:= 0.5*(vp[i-1] + vp[i])
  OD  ;
  vq   );
```

```
PROC trap  = (#to level # INT p, VEC v) VEC :
( INT np = n(p), nq =  UPB v;
  VEC vp = HEAP [0:np] REAL ;
  INT st = ( np=nq ! 1 !: 2*np=nq ! 2 ! error; 0 );
  REAL a = begin OF int, b = end OF int; REAL h = (b-a)/nq;
  FOR i FROM 0 BY st TO nq
  DO REAL s, tj; REAL ti = a + i*h;
     s := kk(ti,tj:=a,v[0])/2;
     FOR j TO nq-1
     DO  s +:= kk(ti,tj+:=h,v[j]) OD ;
     s +:=  kk(ti,tj+h,v[nq])/2;
     vp[i OVER st] := s*h
  OD ;
  vp ) ;

#********************     example 2     *********************************#

PROC cub int = ( VEC vp) VEC :
( INT np = UPB vp; INT nq = 2*np;
  VEC vq = HEAP [0:nq] REAL ;
  vq[0]    := vp[0];
  vq[1]    := (5.0*(vp[0]+3.0*vp[1]-vp[2])+vp[3])/16.0;
  vq[nq-2]:= vp[np-1];
  vq[nq-1]:= (5.0*(vp[np]+3.0*vp[np-1]-vp[np-2])+vp[np-3])/16.0;
  vq[nq]  := vp[np];
  FOR i TO np-2
  DO vq[2*i]   := vp[i];
     vq[2*i+1]:= (-vp[i-1]+9.0*(vp[i]+vp[i+1])-vp[i+2])/16.0
  OD ;
  vq    ) ;

PROC simp  = (#to level # INT p, VEC v) VEC :
(  INT np = n(p), nq =  UPB v;
   VEC vp = HEAP [0:np] REAL ;
   INT st = ( np=nq ! 1 !: 2*np=nq ! 2 ! error; 0 );
   REAL a = begin OF int, b = end OF int, w43 = 4/3, w23 = 2/3;
   REAL h = (b-a)/nq;
   FOR i FROM 0 BY st TO nq
   DO REAL s, tj; REAL ti = a + i*h;
      s := kk(ti,tj:=a,v[0])/3;
      FOR j TO nq-1
      DO  s +:= ( ODD j ! w43 ! w23) * kk(ti,tj+:=h,v[j]) OD ;
      s +:=  kk(ti,tj+h,v[nq])/3;
      vp[i OVER st] := s*h
   OD ;
   vp ) ;

#****************** end of  example 2    ****************************#
```

```
PROC solve directly = ( MAT jacobian, VEC um, rhsm) VOID :
BEGIN      # gaussian elimination #
( 1 UPB jacobian /= UPB rhsm OR 2 UPB jacobian/= UPB rhsm !
 error);
MAT jb= jacobian[ AT 1, AT 1];
INT n = UPB jb;
[1:n,1:n+1] REAL a;
VEC v = a[,n+1]; a[,1:n]:= jb; v:= rhsm[ AT 1];
FOR j TO n
DO INT jp1= j+1; INT pj:= j;
   REAL si,s:= ABS a[j,j];
   FOR i FROM jp1 TO n
   DO ((si:= ABS a[i,j]) >s ! s:=si; pj:=i ) OD ;
   IF  j /= pj
   THEN REAL t;
        FOR k TO n+1
        DO t:= a[pj,k]; a[pj,k]:= a[j,k]; a[j,k]:=t OD
   FI  ;
   s := a[j,j];
   FOR i FROM jp1 TO n
   DO si:= a[i,j]/s;
      FOR k FROM j TO n+1
      DO a[i,k] -:= a[j,k]*si OD
   OD
OD ;
FOR j FROM n BY -1 TO 1
DO v[j] /:= a[j,j];
   FOR i FROM j-1 BY -1 TO 1
   DO v[i] -:= a[i,j]*v[j] OD
OD ;
um:= v[ AT (1 LWB jacobian)]
END # solve directly # ;

PROC evaluate jacobian = ( INT m, VEC um ) MAT :
BEGIN INT nm = n(m);       [0:nm] REAL umd := um;
      VEC qm = q(m,um);    HEAP [0:nm,0:nm] REAL jac;
      FOR i FROM 0 TO nm
      DO REAL delta = max(( um[i]*0.001, 0.001));
         umd[i]  +:= delta;
         jac[,i]  := (qm - q(m,umd))/delta;
         jac[i,i]+:= 1.0;
         umd[i]   := um[i]
      OD ; jac
END # evaluate jacobian # ;
```

```
# PROC mulgrid      =    see text 3.3.2                              #
# PROC solve int eq =    see text 3.3.3                              #

#*****************  global variables     *****************************#

INT n0:= 4; REAL tol:=1.0e-6;
INTERVAL int;
PROC ( REAL , REAL , REAL ) REAL kk;
PROC ( REAL ) REAL forcey;
PROC ( INT , PROC ( REAL ) REAL ) VEC project;
PROC ( VEC ) VEC  restrict;
PROC ( VEC ) VEC  prolongate;  REAL normt;
PROC ( INT , VEC ) VEC q ;    REAL alfa ;

#************   implementation of example 1   ***********************#

 project:=pinject; restrict:=inject;
 prolongate:= lin int;  normt:=  6;  q:=trap;   alfa:=2;

#************   implementation of example 2   ***********************#

 project:=pinject; restrict:=inject;
 prolongate:= cub int;  normt:= 24;  q:=simp;   alfa:=4;

#*******************************************************************#

#*****************    end of library    *****************************#

PR prog PR SKIP
END
```

TEXT 3.4. An ALGOL 68 program for the automatic solution of Fredholm equations of the second kind, in which the linear system is iteratively solved by a multiple grid method.

Example 1: Approximation of the integral by the trapezoidal rule.

Example 2: Approximation of the integral by Simpson's rule.

CHAPTER 4

MULTIPLE GRID METHODS FOR INTEGRAL EQUATIONS IN POTENTIAL THEORY

In this chapter we discuss the numerical solution of the Dirichlet problem for Laplace's equation. We will use the classical approach of representation of the solution by means of a singularity distribution on the boundary of the domain. This approach has recently been advocated anew by BREBBIA [4,5] and JASWON & SYMM [11], and is in widespread use for aerodynamic computations. A disadvantage of this approach is, as noted by JASWON & SYMM in the introduction in [11], that "unfortunately no rigorous error analysis of the numerical solutions is available". In this chapter we partly fill this gap. We supply the error analysis of an approximation for the solution of the two-dimensional (2-D) Dirichlet problem.

The solution, which is a harmonic function, is represented as a double layer potential. Applying the Dirichlet conditions on the boundary one obtains a Fredholm integral equation of the second kind for the doublet distribution μ. In this chapter we shall approximate μ by a piecewise constant function μ_N. To supply an error analysis we first discuss the regularity of the principal value of the double layer potential in Section 4.1. Assuming the boundary to satisfy a certain smoothness condition and μ to be essentially bounded we obtain a result concerning the regularity of the principal value (in 2-D it turns out to be more regular than in 3-D). This result is used in Sections 4.2 and 4.3. In Section 4.2 we give the error analysis of the approximate solution. The numerical method results in a non-sparse system of equations, that is solved by a multiple grid iterative process. In Section 4.3 we estimate the reduction factor of this process. We illustrate the results of these sections with the calculation of non-circulatory potential flow around a Kármán-Trefftz aerofoil. The corresponding boundary does not satisfy the smoothness condition assumed in Section 4.1, because of the corner at the trailing edge. In Section 4.4 we remove the corner by a mapping to obtain a boundary that satisfies our smoothness assumption. For some examples the theoretical estimates of Section 4.3 are found to be too pessimistic. In Section 4.5 we apply our multiple grid method to circulatory flow. The trailing edge angle is not removed, so that the theorems of Sections 4.1 – 4.3 do not hold. However, the rate of convergence of the multiple grid process turns out to be quite satisfactory. In this section we measure the error between the analytical and numerical solution by means of a suitable metric, i.e. the supremum norm over the boundary apart from a fixed, small neighbourhood near the trailing edge, that removes the influence of the singular behaviour of the solution near the trailing edge. By experiments we show that the numerical solution converges with respect to this metric.

4.1. REGULARITY RESULT

The solution of the Dirichlet problem for Laplace's equation in two and three dimensions can be represented as a double layer potential, respectively:

$$\phi_d^{(2)}(\zeta) = \frac{1}{2\pi}\int_S \mu(z)\,\frac{\partial}{\partial n_z}\log|r_{z\zeta}|\,dS_z, \qquad \zeta \notin S,$$

$$\phi_d^{(3)}(\zeta) = \frac{1}{4\pi}\int_S \mu(z)\,\frac{\partial}{\partial n_z}1/|r_{z\zeta}|\,dS_z, \qquad \zeta \notin S,$$

where n_z is the outward normal to the surface S at the point z, $r_{z\zeta} = z - \zeta$ and $\mu(\cdot)$ is called the *doublet distribution*. These potentials are discontinuous across the surface. We denote the principal value of $\phi_d(\zeta)$ by

$$\bar{\phi}_d^{(m)}(\zeta) = \frac{2^{1-m}}{\pi}\int_S \mu(z)\,\frac{\cos(n_z, z-\zeta)}{|r_{z\zeta}|^{m-1}}\,dS_z, \quad \zeta \in S,$$

where m = 2,3 for the two- and three-dimensional case, respectively. Assuming S to be a Lyapunov surface and μ to be essentially bounded, GÜNTER [9, p.49] proved that $\bar{\phi}_d^{(3)} \in H^{0,\alpha}(S)$, where $H^{k,\alpha}(S)$ denotes the class of continuous functions whose derivatives of order k satisfy a uniform Hölder condition with exponent α. In this section we prove that in the two-dimensional case $\bar{\phi}_d^{(2)} \in H^{1,\alpha}(S)$.

The interior Dirichlet problem has an important application in aerodynamics, namely the calculation of potential flow around aerofoils (2-D) and wings (3-D). As we shall see later, in the 2-D problem the doublet distribution μ is the solution of the following Fredholm equation of the second kind:

$$\mu(\zeta) + \frac{1}{\pi} \int_S \mu(z) \frac{\cos(n_z, z-\zeta)}{|z-\zeta|} \, dS_z = -2\mathcal{U}\cdot\zeta, \qquad \zeta \in S,$$

where $\mathcal{U}$ is the velocity vector of the undisturbed flow and $\mathcal{U}\cdot\zeta$ denotes the usual inner product in $\mathbb{R}^2$. In this section we will show that the linear integral operator occurring in this equation is a bounded mapping from $L_\infty(S)$ into $H^{1,\alpha}(S)$, with $L_\infty(S)$ the Banach space of essentially bounded functions. This result is applied in Section 4.2 and 4.3. For aerodynamics it is of particular interest that an approximate solution belonging to $H^{1,\alpha}(S)$ can be obtained by means of the numerical method of Section 4.2, provided the aerofoil is sufficiently smooth (see Remark 4.2.3).

First, we give some definitions which have been taken from GÜNTER [9]. Let $D \subset \mathbb{R}^2$ be a bounded simply connected open set with boundary S and closure $\bar{D}$.

<u>DEFINITION 4.1.1.</u> $C^k(D)(C^k(\bar{D}))$ denotes the class of functions which are k times continuously differentiable in $D(\bar{D})$.

<u>DEFINITION 4.1.2.</u> $C^{k,\alpha}(D)(C^{k,\alpha}(\bar{D}))$ denotes the subclass of functions in $C^k(D)(C^k(\bar{D}))$, whose derivatives of order k satisfy a uniform Hölder condition with exponent α, $0 < \alpha < 1$.

<u>DEFINITION 4.1.3.</u> $L^{k,\alpha}$ $(k \geq 1)$ denotes the class of rectifiable contours S in 2-dimensional Euclidean space with the property that for every point P on S there exists a number $\varepsilon > 0$ such that the part Σ of S within the circle $B_{\varepsilon,P}$ of radius ε and centre P, for the orientation as given in Figure 4.1.1 of the axes of the coordinate system (x,y), admits a representation

$$y = F(x), \qquad x \in \bar{D}_{\varepsilon,P},$$

where $F \in C^{k,\alpha}(\bar{D}_{\varepsilon,P})$, $\bar{D}_{\varepsilon,P}$ the projection of the part of S within $B_{\varepsilon,P}$ on the line $y = 0$.

We give an illustration of Definition 4.1.3 in the following figure.

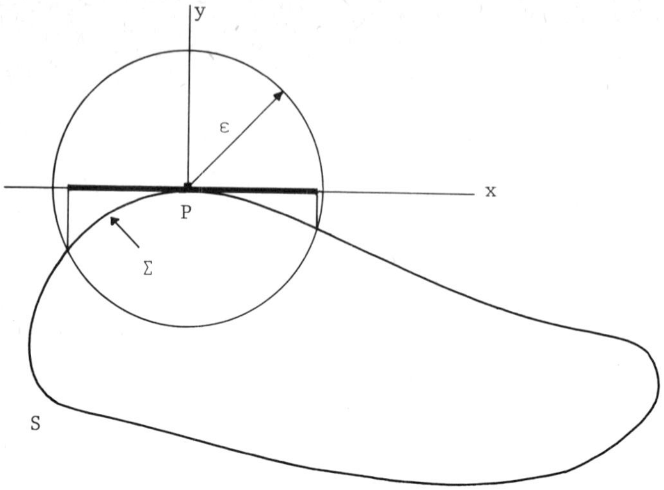

Figure 4.1.1. Illustration of Definition 4.1.3.
($\bar{D}_{\varepsilon,P}$ is given by ▬▬▬).

We remark that the class $L^{k,\alpha}$ is equivalent with the class of Jordan curves, defined by the parametric equations $x = X(t)$, $y = Y(t)$ with $X,Y \in C^{k,\alpha}[0,1]$ and $\dot{X}^2 + \dot{Y}^2 \neq 0$ (see GOLUSIN [8, chapt. X]).

DEFINITION 4.1.4. $H^{k,\alpha}(S)$ denotes the class of functions f defined on S with the property that the function $\hat{f}$ defined by

$$\hat{f}(x) = f(x,F(x)), \qquad x \in \bar{D}_{\varepsilon,P},$$

with $F(x)$ and $\bar{D}_{\varepsilon,P}$ as in Definition 4.1.3, belongs to the class $C^{k,\alpha}(\bar{D}_{\varepsilon,P})$.

REMARK 4.1.1. Let $S \in L^{k,\alpha}$ with $k \geq 2$ and let $z,\zeta \in S$. Then

$$\lim_{\zeta\to z} \frac{2\cos(n_z, z-\zeta)}{|z-\zeta|} = \kappa(z),$$

where $\kappa(z)$ is the curvature at z. Moreover, κ belongs to the space $H^{k-2,\alpha}(S)$.

PROOF. Let (ξ,η) be a local coordinate system about a certain point $P \in S$ (see Figure 4.1.1). By Definition 4.1.3 the points z and ζ may be represented by $(x,F(x))$ and $(\xi,F(\xi))$, respectively. Now

$$\lim_{\zeta\to z} \frac{2\cos(n_z, z-\zeta)}{|z-\zeta|} = \lim_{\xi\to x} \frac{2\{F(x) - F(\xi) + (\xi-x)F'(x)\}}{\{(x-\xi)^2 + (F(x) - F(\xi))^2\}\{1 + (F'(x))^2\}^{\frac{1}{2}}}.$$

Since

$$F(x) - F(\xi) + (\xi-x)F'(x) = -(\xi-x)^2 \int_0^1 t\, F''(\xi + (x-\xi)t)dt$$

and

$$F(x) - F(\xi) = (x-\xi) \int_0^1 F'(\xi + (x-\xi)t)dt$$

we obtain

$$\lim_{\zeta\to z} \frac{2\cos(n_z, z-\zeta)}{|z-\zeta|} = F''(x)/\{1 + (F'(x))^2\}^{3/2},$$

which is the definition of the curvature $\kappa(z)$. Since $F \in C^{k,\alpha}(\bar{D}_{\varepsilon,P})$ it follows that $\kappa \in H^{k-2,\alpha}(S)$. □

For the two-dimensional case the potential due to a doublet distribution μ along the boundary can be written as follows:

(4.1.1) $$\phi_d^{(2)}(\zeta) = \frac{1}{2\pi} \int_S \mu(z) \frac{\cos(n_z, z-\zeta)}{|z-\zeta|}\, dS_z, \qquad \zeta \notin S.$$

From now on the superscript (2) will be deleted because only the two-dimensional case will be considered.

LEMMA 4.1.1. *Let* $S \in L^{2,\alpha}$ *and* $\mu \in H^{1,\alpha}(S)$. *If* ζ *approaches* S *we have* (Plemelj-Privalov formulae):

(4.1.2a) $$\phi_d^+(\zeta) = -\tfrac{1}{2}\mu(\zeta) + \bar{\phi}_d(\zeta),$$

(4.1.2b) $$\phi_d^-(\zeta) = \tfrac{1}{2}\mu(\zeta) + \bar{\phi}_d(\zeta),$$

with

(4.1.2c) $$\bar{\phi}_d(\zeta) = \frac{1}{2\pi} \int_S \mu(z) \frac{\cos(n_z, z-\zeta)}{|z-\zeta|}\, dS_z, \quad \zeta \in S,$$

where ϕ_d^+ *and* ϕ_d^- *denote the limit from the outer and inner side, respectively.*

PROOF. See MUSCHELISCHWILI [15, pp.36-42, p.52]. □

For $z = \zeta$ the kernel in (4.1.2c) is defined by its limit value, which is the curvature at ζ (cf. Remark 4.1.1). Thus the integral in (4.1.2c) may be interpreted as a proper integral.

The main result of this section is the following theorem. The proof of this theorem leans strongly on 3-D results given by GÜNTER [9, p.312], who has proven the following theorem: *let* $S \in L^{2,\alpha}$ *and* $\mu \in H^{0,\alpha}(S)$, *then* $\bar{\phi}_d^{(3)} \in H^{1,\alpha}(S)$. The reason why we cannot apply this theorem is that we only assume μ to be essentially bounded, because of the numerical application to be discussed later. We define this class of functions on a rectifiable contour, because PRIWALOW [17] has shown that for such a contour measurability and summability can be introduced in the same way as for a straight line.

DEFINITION 4.1.5. $L_\infty(S)$ denotes the Banach space of essentially bounded functions on a rectifiable contour S which are measurable with respect to S. The associated norm is

$$\|\mu\|_\infty = \operatorname*{ess\,sup}_{z \in S} |\mu(z)|.$$

It is noteworthy to remark that if $S \in L^{2,\alpha}$, then S is rectifiable.

THEOREM 4.1.2. *Let* $S \in L^{2,\alpha}$ *and* $\mu \in L_\infty(S)$; *then* $\bar{\phi}_d \in H^{1,\alpha}(S)$.

PROOF. Let (ξ,η) be a local coordinate system about a certain point $P \in S$ of the type given by Fig. 4.1.1. Using Definition 4.1.3 we split the boundary into two parts Σ and $S-\Sigma$. Let $\zeta \in \Sigma_0$, being the part of Σ within the circle with radius $\varepsilon/2$ and centre P. For (4.1.2c) we obtain

$$\bar{\phi}_d(\zeta) = \frac{1}{2\pi}\int_{S-\Sigma} \mu(z)\,\frac{\cos(n_z, z-\zeta)}{|z-\zeta|}\,dS_z + \frac{1}{2\pi}\int_{\Sigma} \mu(z)\,\frac{\cos(n_z, z-\zeta)}{|z-\zeta|}\,dS_z.$$

In the first integral $|z-\zeta| \neq 0$. If we replace ζ by $(\xi, F(\xi))$ we obtain a function of ξ which has bounded and continuous derivatives up to order 2 (since $S \in L^{2,\alpha}$); hence the first integral certainly belongs to the class $H^{1,\alpha}(S)$. We proceed to establish that the second integral also belongs to $H^{1,\alpha}(S)$. We denote the coordinates of the point ζ by ξ,η and those of the integration point z by x,y. Substituting $\eta = F(\xi)$ and $y = F(x)$ we obtain

$$I_2 \equiv \int_{\Sigma} \mu(z)\,\frac{\cos(n_z, z-\zeta)}{|z-\zeta|}\,dS_z = \int_{\bar{D}_{\varepsilon,P}} \mu(x)\,\frac{F(x) - F(\xi) + (\xi-x)F'(x)}{\{(x-\xi)^2 + (F(x) - F(\xi))^2\}}\,dx.$$

We define the following functions:

$$\psi_1(\xi,x) = \int_0^1 F'(\xi + (x-\xi)t)dt$$

and

$$\psi_2(\xi,x) = \int_0^1 tF''(\xi + (x-\xi)t)dt.$$

Integrating by parts, we obtain:

$$F(x) - F(\xi) + (\xi-x)F'(x) = -(\xi-x)^2\psi_2(\xi,x) \tag{4.1.3}$$

and

$$F(x) - F(\xi) = (x-\xi)\psi_1(\xi,x). \tag{4.1.4}$$

Hence, the second integral becomes

$$I_2 = -\int_{\bar{D}_{\varepsilon,P}} \mu(x) \frac{\psi_2(\xi,x)}{(1+\psi_1^2(\xi,x))} dx. \tag{4.1.5}$$

Assuming $\|\mu\|_\infty < A$ we have to prove that:

$$\left|\frac{dI_2}{d\xi}\right| < CA, \tag{4.1.6}$$

and

$$\left|\frac{d}{d\xi} I_2(\xi_1) - \frac{d}{d\xi} I_2(\xi_2)\right| < CA|\xi_1-\xi_2|^\alpha, \quad \forall \xi_1,\xi_2 \in \bar{D}_{\varepsilon,P}. \tag{4.1.7}$$

First, we show that

$$|\psi_2(\xi_1,x) - \psi_2(\xi_2,x)| \le C|\xi_1-\xi_2|^\alpha.$$

Indeed, since $F'' \in C^{0,\alpha}(\bar{D}_{\varepsilon,P})$, we have

$$|\psi_2(\xi_1,x) - \psi_2(\xi_2,x)| = \left|\int_0^1 t\,\{F''(\xi_1 + (x-\xi_1)t) - F''(\xi_2 + (x-\xi_2)t)\}dt\right| \le$$

$$\le \int_0^1 |F''(\xi_1 + (x-\xi_1)t) - F''(\xi_2 + (x-\xi_2)t)|dt \le$$

$$\le C\int_0^1 |\xi_1 + (x-\xi_1)t-\xi_2-(x-\xi_2)t|^\alpha dt \le C'|\xi_1-\xi_2|^\alpha.$$

Next, we investigate the function

$$(4.1.8) \qquad R(\xi,x) \equiv \frac{\psi_2(\xi,x)}{1+\psi_1^2(\xi,x)}.$$

Since ψ_2 is bounded, R is bounded too. We shall now prove the following inequalities:

$$(4.1.9) \qquad \left|\frac{\partial R}{\partial \xi}\right| < \frac{C}{|\xi-x|^{1-\alpha}} \qquad \text{for } \xi \to x,$$

$$(4.1.10) \qquad \left|\frac{\partial^2 R}{\partial \xi^2}\right| < \frac{C}{|\xi-x|^{2-\alpha}} \qquad \text{for } \xi \to x.$$

Differentiating R we obtain:

$$(4.1.11) \qquad \frac{\partial R}{\partial \xi} = \frac{\partial \psi_2}{\partial \xi}(1+\psi_1^2)^{-1} - 2(1+\psi_1^2)^{-2}\psi_1\frac{\partial \psi_1}{\partial \xi}\psi_2.$$

It can be easily proven that $|\frac{\partial \psi_1}{\partial \xi}| < c_0$. Since $|1+\psi_1^2| > 1$, $|\psi_1| < c_1$ and $|\psi_2| < c_2$ (with c_0, c_1, c_2 certain constants that depend on F) it follows that

$$\left|\frac{\partial R}{\partial \xi}\right| < \left|\frac{\partial \psi_2}{\partial \xi}\right| + 2c_0c_1c_2.$$

Inequality (4.1.9) will have been proven when we have shown that

$$(4.1.12) \qquad \left|\frac{\partial \psi_2}{\partial \xi}\right| < \frac{C}{|\xi-x|^{1-\alpha}}.$$

From (4.1.3) we obtain

$$(4.1.13) \qquad \frac{\partial \psi_2}{\partial \xi} = 2\,\frac{\psi_2}{(x-\xi)} + \frac{F'(\xi)-F'(x)}{(x-\xi)^2}.$$

Since

$$F'(\xi) - F'(x) = -(x-\xi)\int_0^1 F''(\xi+(x-\xi)t)\,dt,$$

it follows that

$$\frac{\partial \psi_2}{\partial \xi} = \left\{2\int_0^1 tF''(\xi+(x-\xi)t)\,dt - \int_0^1 F''(\xi+(x-\xi)t)\,dt\right\}/(x-\xi) =$$

$$= \frac{1}{(x-\xi)}\int_0^1 \left\{F''(\xi+(x-\xi)\sqrt{t}) - F''(\xi+(x-\xi)t)\right\}dt.$$

Hence

$$\left|\frac{\partial\psi_2}{\partial\xi}\right| \le \frac{c}{|x-\xi|}\int_0^1 |\xi + (x-\xi)\sqrt{t} - \xi - (x-\xi)t|^\alpha \, dt \le$$

$$\le \frac{c}{|x-\xi|^{1-\alpha}}\int_0^1 |\sqrt{t}-t|^\alpha \, dt \le$$

$$\le \frac{C}{|x-\xi|^{1-\alpha}},$$

which establishes (4.1.9). We continue with (4.1.10). Using (4.1.9) and (4.1.12) we obtain by another differentiation of R the estimate:

$$\left|\frac{\partial^2 R}{\partial\xi^2}\right| < \left|\frac{\partial^2\psi_2}{\partial\xi^2}\right| + \frac{c_3}{|x-\xi|^{1-\alpha}} + c_4.$$

Therefore it sufficies to show that

$$\left|\frac{\partial^2\psi_2}{\partial\xi^2}\right| < \frac{c}{|x-\xi|^{2-\alpha}}.$$

Differentiating (4.1.13) we obtain:

$$\frac{\partial^2\psi_2}{\partial\xi^2} = \frac{2\psi_2}{(x-\xi)^2} + \frac{2}{(x-\xi)}\frac{\partial\psi_2}{\partial\xi} + \frac{2}{(x-\xi)^3}\{F'(\xi) - F'(x)\} + \frac{F''(\xi)}{(x-\xi)^2} =$$

$$= \frac{3}{(x-\xi)}\frac{\partial\psi_2}{\partial\xi} + \frac{1}{(x-\xi)^3}\{F'(\xi) - F'(x)\} + \frac{F''(\xi)}{(x-\xi)^2} =$$

$$= \frac{3}{(x-\xi)}\frac{\partial\psi_2}{\partial\xi} + \frac{1}{(x-\xi)^2}\left[F''(\xi) - \int_0^1 F''(\xi + (x-\xi)t)dt\right].$$

Because of the mean value theorem the expression within square brackets is equal to

$$F''(\xi) - F''(\xi + (x-\xi)t^*), \quad \text{for some } t^* \in [0,1].$$

Since $F'' \in C^{0,\alpha}(\bar{D}_{\varepsilon,P})$ and $\left|\frac{\partial\psi_2}{\partial\xi}\right| < \frac{c}{|x-\xi|^{1-\alpha}}$ it follows that

$$\left|\frac{\partial^2\psi_2}{\partial\xi^2}\right| < \frac{c}{|x-\xi|^{2-\alpha}},$$

which establishes (4.1.10). Turning to (4.1.6), we consider the integral

$$\frac{dI_2}{d\xi}(\xi) = \int_{\bar{D}_{\varepsilon,P}} \mu(x) \frac{\partial R}{\partial \xi}(\xi,x)dx.$$

Without loss of generality we can take $\bar{D}_{\varepsilon,P}$ equal to $[0,1]$. Since $\|\mu\|_\infty \leq A$ it follows that

$$\left|\frac{dI_2}{d\xi}\right| \leq A \int_0^1 \left|\frac{\partial R}{\partial \xi}(\xi,x)\right| dx.$$

Using estimate (4.1.9) we conclude that the singularity in $\frac{\partial R}{\partial \xi}$ is integrable. Hence, (4.1.6) holds. We proceed to establish (4.1.7). Let $\delta = |\xi_1-\xi_2|$, then

$$\begin{aligned}
(4.1.14) \quad \left|\frac{dI_2}{d\xi}(\xi_1) - \frac{dI_2}{d\xi}(\xi_2)\right| &\leq A \int_0^1 \left|\frac{\partial R}{\partial \xi}(\xi_1,x) - \frac{\partial R}{\partial \xi}(\xi_2,x)\right| dx \leq \\
&\leq A \int_{\xi_1-2\delta}^{\xi_1+2\delta} \left|\frac{\partial R}{\partial \xi}(\xi_2,x)\right| dx + A \int_{\xi_1-2\delta}^{\xi_1+2\delta} \left|\frac{\partial R}{\partial \xi}(\xi_1,x)\right| dx + \\
&+ A \int_0^{\xi_1-2\delta} \left|\frac{\partial R}{\partial \xi}(\xi_1,x) - \frac{\partial R}{\partial \xi}(\xi_2,x)\right| dx + \\
&+ A \int_{\xi_1+2\delta}^1 \left|\frac{\partial R}{\partial \xi}(\xi_1,x) - \frac{\partial R}{\partial \xi}(\xi_2,x)\right| dx.
\end{aligned}$$

Because of inequality (4.1.9) we obtain for the second integral on the right-hand side of (4.1.14)

$$\int_{\xi_1-2\delta}^{\xi_1+2\delta} \left|\frac{\partial R}{\partial \xi}(\xi_1)\right| dx < \int_{\xi_1-2\delta}^{\xi_1+2\delta} |\xi_1-x|^{\alpha-1} dx < c(2\delta)^\alpha.$$

Since the interval $|\xi_1-x| < 2\delta$ is contained in the circle $|\xi_2-x| < 3\delta$ we obtain for the first integral the estimate $c(3\delta)^\alpha$. Therefore, the sum of the first two integrals is less than $c\delta^\alpha$ for some c.

Finally, we have to estimate the last two integrals of (4.1.14). For $x \notin [\xi_1,\xi_2]$ the mean value theorem yields

$$\frac{\partial R}{\partial \xi}(\xi_1,x) - \frac{\partial R}{\partial \xi}(\xi_2,x) = (\xi_1-\xi_2) \frac{\partial^2 R}{\partial \xi^2}(\xi^*,x),$$

where ξ^* denotes some point of the interval $[\xi_1,\xi_2]$. From inequality (4.1.10) we obtain

$$\left|\frac{\partial R}{\partial \xi}(\xi_1,x) - \frac{\partial R}{\partial \xi}(\xi_2,x)\right| < \delta c|\xi^*-x|^{\alpha-2},$$

so that for the third integral the following estimate is obtained:

$$c\delta \int_0^{\xi_1-2\delta} (\xi^*-x)^{\alpha-2}\,dx = \frac{c\delta}{\alpha-1}[(\xi^*-\xi_1+2\delta)^{\alpha-1} - \xi^{*\alpha-1}] < \bar{c}\,\delta^{\alpha}.$$

In the same way we obtain a similar estimate for the last integral. Hence, the left-hand side of (4.1.14) is less than a number of the form $c\delta^{\alpha}$. By definition $\delta = |\xi_1-\xi_2|$ and thus the inequality (4.1.7) has been proven. This completes the proof of Theorem 4.1.2. □

In the case of an interior Dirichlet-problem the boundary value ϕ_d^- is prescribed and the solution ϕ_d follows from (4.1.1) as soon as the doublet distribution μ has been determined from equation (4.1.2b). Let the integral operator in (4.1.2c) be denoted symbolically by K:

$$\text{(4.1.15)} \qquad K\mu(\zeta) = \frac{-1}{\pi}\int_S \mu(z)\,\frac{\cos(n_z, z-\zeta)}{|z-\zeta|}\,dS_z, \qquad \zeta \in S.$$

From Theorem 4.1.2 it follows that $K\mu \in H^{1,\alpha}(S)$ if $S \in L^{2,\alpha}$ and $\mu \in L_\infty(S)$. We conclude that the operator K maps from the Banach space $L_\infty(S)$ into the class $H^{1,\alpha}(S)$, which is a Banach space too if it is equipped with the following norm:

$$\|f\|_{1,\alpha} = \sum_{\ell=0}^{1} \|D^{\ell}f\|_{\alpha},$$

where D denotes the differentiation in the tangential direction and

$$\|f\|_{\alpha} = \|f\|_{\infty} + \sup_{z_1,z_2\in S} \frac{|f(z_1) - f(z_2)|}{|z_1-z_2|^{\alpha}}.$$

Since K is a linear operator we obtain directly from Theorem 4.1.2:

<u>COROLLARY 4.1.3</u>. *Let* $S \in L^{2,\alpha}$. *Then the operator* K *mapping from* $L_\infty(S)$ *into* $H^{1,\alpha}(S)$ *satisfies:*

$$\|K\mu\|_{1,\alpha} \le C\|\mu\|_{\infty}, \qquad \textit{for all } \mu \in L_\infty(S).$$

We note that the space $H^{1,\alpha}(S)$ is compactly imbedded in the space $L_\infty(S)$ (see KRASNOSELSKII [13, p.4]). From this property and the previous corollary follow:

COROLLARY 4.1.4. *Let* $S \in L^{2,\alpha}$. *Then the operator* K *mapping from* $L_\infty(S)$ *into* $L_\infty(S)$ *is compact.*

REMARK 4.1.2. From the Fredholm alternative theorem for compact operators it follows that equation (4.1.2b) has a unique solution for each boundary function $\bar{\phi}_d \in L_\infty(S)$ if $S \in L^{2,\alpha}$ (see also ZABREYKO [22, p.218]). In addition, the operator $(I-K)^{-1}$ is bounded on the space $L_\infty(S)$,

$$\|(I-K)^{-1}\|_\infty < C.$$

COROLLARY 4.1.5. *Let* $S \in L^{2,\alpha}$ *and* $\bar{\phi}_d \in H^{1,\alpha}(S)$. *Then the solution of* (4.1.2b) *belongs to* $H^{1,\alpha}(S)$.

PROOF. From Remark 4.1.2 we have $\mu \in L_\infty(S)$. But (4.1.2b) can be written as

$$\mu = 2\bar{\phi}_d + K\mu.$$

By Theorem 4.1.2 it follows that the right-hand side belongs to $H^{1,\alpha}(S)$. □

4.2. ERROR ANALYSIS

The classical method described in the previous section is used to solve the Dirichlet problem

(4.2.1a) $\quad \Delta\phi = 0 \quad \text{in } D \subset \mathbb{R}^2,$

with the boundary condition

(4.2.1b) $\quad \phi(\zeta) = a(\zeta)$

along the boundary S. The solution is given by the double layer potential ϕ_d (4.1.1) if the doublet distribution μ is determined from the following integral equation

(4.2.2) $\quad (I-K)\mu = 2a,$

where K is the integral operator defined by (4.1.15).

ASSUMPTION 4.2.1. *The boundary function* $a \in H^{1,\alpha}(S)$.

We approximate μ by a piecewise constant function μ_N. We shall supply error bounds for

$$(4.2.3) \qquad \|\mu-\mu_N\|_\infty,$$

$$(4.2.4) \qquad \max_{1\le i\le N} |\mu(\zeta_i) - \mu_N(\zeta_i)|,$$

and

$$(4.2.5) \qquad |\phi_d(\zeta) - \hat{\phi}_d(\zeta)|, \qquad \zeta \in D,$$

where $\zeta_1,\ldots,\zeta_N$ are the collocation points to be chosen, and

$$(4.2.6) \qquad \hat{\phi}_d(\zeta) = \frac{1}{2\pi}\int_S \mu_N(\zeta)\, \frac{\cos(n_z, z-\zeta)}{|z-\zeta|}\, dS_z, \qquad \zeta \in D.$$

First we discuss the convergence of a sequence of approximations to the unique solution of (4.2.2). We divide the boundary S into N segments S_i, such that $S = \bigcup_{i=1}^{N} S_i$ and $S_i \cap S_j = \emptyset$, $i \neq j$. The begin- and end-points of the i-th segment are z_{i-1} and z_i. The points z_i are called *nodal points* and are given by the global coordinates (X_i,Y_i). The function μ is approximated by a piecewise constant function μ_N which is defined as follows:

$$\mu_N(\zeta) = \sum_{i=1}^{N} \alpha_i u_i(\zeta),$$

with

$$u_i(\zeta) = \begin{cases} 1, & \zeta \in S_i, \\ 0, & \zeta \notin S_i. \end{cases}$$

The resulting equation is solved by a collocation method. The collocation points ζ_i, $i = 1,2,\ldots,N$, are taken to be the mid-points of the segments S_i, or more precisely:

DEFINITION 4.2.1. Let (x,y) be a local coordinate system in the sense of Definition 4.1.3 about ζ_i. Then the local coordinates of z_i are given by $(x_i,F(x_i))$. The collocation point ζ_i should be chosen such that $x_{i-1}+x_i = 0$.

Let X_N be the finite dimensional space of piecewise constant functions spanned by $u_1, u_2, \ldots, u_N$. For our application we need an *interpolatory projection* operator T_N from a Banach space X onto X_N. We have to be careful with respect to our choice of X. It is not possible to choose $X = L_\infty(S)$ because pointwise operations are not defined on elements of $L_\infty(S)$. We note that it is possible to define a linear mapping from the space C(S) of continuous functions on S (with the supremum norm $\|\cdot\|_\infty$) to X_N, but in this case the mapping is *not* a projection operator in C(S) because X_N is not a subspace of C(S). We choose X to be the space of regulated functions (classical term: functions with only discontinuities of the "first kind"), which is a Banach space when considered as a subspace of $L_\infty(S)$ (see DIEUDONNÉ [7, p.145 and p.317]).

DEFINITION 4.2.2. The space of regulated functions R(S) is the space of functions f defined on a rectifiable contour S with the property that the function $\hat{f}$, defined by

$$\hat{f}(x) = f(x, F(x)), \qquad x \in D_{\varepsilon,P},$$

with F(x) and $D_{\varepsilon,P}$ as in Definition 4.1.3, has one-sided limits at every point of S, i.e. for all $x \in D_{\varepsilon,P}$ the limits $\lim_{h\to 0} \hat{f}(x+h)$ and $\lim_{h\to 0} \hat{f}(x-h)$ exist. The associated norm is $\|\cdot\|_\infty$.

By this definition the following inclusion relations hold:

$$C(S) \subset R(S) \subset L_\infty(S).$$

Hence, Theorem 4.1.2 also holds if $\mu \in R(S)$ (or $\mu \in C(S)$).

Let the global coordinates of collocation point ζ_i be (X_i^*, Y_i^*) and let the local coordinates of $z \in S_i$ be given by (x,F(x)) with F as in Definition 4.1.3. We define the interpolatory projection operator T_N: $R(S) \to X_N$ as follows:

$$(4.2.7) \qquad T_N f(\zeta) = \sum_{i=1}^{N} d_i u_i(\zeta),$$

where $d_i = \frac{1}{2}[\lim_{h\to 0} \tilde{f}(h) + \lim_{h\to 0} \tilde{f}(-h)]$ with $\tilde{f}(x) = f(X_i^* + x\cos\nu - F(x)\sin\nu, Y_i^* + x\sin\nu + F(x)\cos\nu)$; and ν is the angle between the local and global x-axis (see Figure 4.2.1).

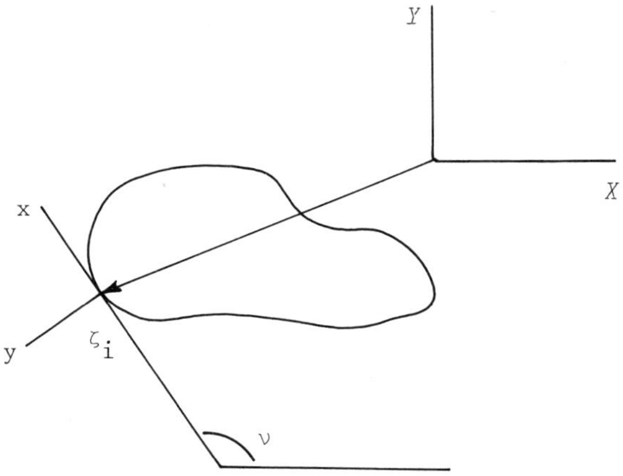

Figure 4.2.1. (X,Y) - global coordinate system,
(x,y) - local coordinate system about ζ_i.

LEMMA 4.2.1. *The mappings* T_N *and* $I - T_N$ *are bounded on* $R(S)$.

PROOF. For all $f \in R(S)$ we have

$$\sup_{f \in R(S)} \|T_N f\|_\infty = \max_{1 \le i \le N} |f(\zeta_i)| \le \|f\|_\infty. \qquad \square$$

Let h_N be a measure of the mesh-size defined by:

$$h_N = \max_{1 \le i \le N} |z_i - z_{i-1}|.$$

We assume that the partition of the boundary is such that $\lim_{N \to \infty} h_N = 0$.

LEMMA 4.2.2. *Let* $S \in L^{2,\alpha}$ *and* $f \in H^{1,\alpha}(S)$; *then*

$$\|(I - T_N) f\|_\infty \le C\, h_N \|f\|_{1,\alpha} \quad \textit{as } N \to \infty.$$

PROOF. Draw a circle with centre ζ_i and radius h_N. The proof follows from Definition 4.1.4. $\square$

For a given N an approximate solution of equation (4.2.2) is obtained by solving:

$$(4.2.8)\qquad (I - T_N K)\mu_N = 2T_N a, \qquad \mu_N \in X_N.$$

REMARK 4.2.1. In aerodynamics this collocation method has become very popular because $T_N K\mu_N$ can be easily calculated. In the two-dimensional case angles have to be computed.

REMARK 4.2.2. As a consequence of Theorem 4.1.2 an approximation in the space $H^{1,\alpha}(S)$ can be obtained by a single iteration (Nyström interpolation):

$$(4.2.9)\qquad \tilde{\mu}_N = 2a + K\mu_N,$$

where μ_N is the solution of (4.2.8). It is easily verified that

$$\tilde{\mu}_N = 2a + KT_N\tilde{\mu}_N.$$

For the case that K represents a sufficiently regular integral operator the convergence properties of $\tilde{\mu}_N$ as $N \to \infty$, are discussed by SLOAN [18].

REMARK 4.2.3. In practice aerofoils are given by a data-set of points $\{x_i,y_i\}_{i=1}^{M}$. Usually a continuous boundary is obtained by a polygon connecting the points of the data-set. However, this polygon does not belong to the class $L^{2,\alpha}$ and a single iteration does not yield an approximation in the space $H^{1,\alpha}(S)$. Therefore, if one wants to have the approximate solution $\tilde{\mu}_N$ in $H^{1,\alpha}(S)$, it is necessary to construct a smoother boundary through the points $\{x_i,y_i\}$, e.g. a cubic spline approximation so that $S \in L^{2,\alpha}$, except for a neighbourhood of the trailing edge.

LEMMA 4.2.3. *Let the finite-dimensional subspace* $X_N \subset L_\infty(S)$ *be sufficiently large (i.e. the mesh-size of the discretization is sufficiently small) and let* $S \in L^{2,\alpha}$. *From the existence of a bounded inverse of* $I - K$ *on* $L_\infty(S)$ *follow:*

$$(I - T_N K)^{-1} \quad \textit{exists on } L_\infty(S)$$

and

$$C_1 \equiv \sup_{n\geq N} \| (I - T_n K)^{-1} \|_{L_\infty(S) \to L_\infty(S)} < \infty.$$

PROOF. For $f \in L_\infty(S)$ we have by Lemma 4.2.2 and Corollary 4.1.3

$$\| (I - T_N)Kf\|_\infty \leq c\, h_N \|Kf\|_{1,\alpha} \leq c\, h_N \|f\|_\infty .$$

But then $\|K - T_N K\|_{L_\infty(S) \to L_\infty(S)} \to 0$ as $N \to \infty$ and existence and boundedness of $I - T_N K$ on $L_\infty(S)$ follow from Neumann's theorem. See also PRENTER [16, p.574]. □

LEMMA 4.2.4. *Let* $S \in L^{2,\alpha}$ *and* $f \in H^{1,\alpha}(S)$; *then*

$$\left| \int_{S_i} \{f(z) - f(\zeta_i)\} dS_z \right| \leq C_2 h_N^{2+\alpha} \|f\|_{1,\alpha}, \qquad \textit{as } N \to \infty.$$

PROOF. Let (x,y) be a local coordinate system in the sense of Definition 4.1.3 about the collocation point ζ_i. We denote the coordinates of the point ζ_i by (ξ,η) and those of the integration point z by (x,y). Using Definition 4.1.4 we can represent $f(z) - f(\zeta_i)$ by

$$\hat{f}(x) - \hat{f}(\xi) = (x-\xi)\hat{f}'(\xi) + (x-\xi) \int_0^1 \{\hat{f}'(\xi + (x-\xi)t) - \hat{f}'(\xi)\} dt.$$

We recall that ζ_i is the mid-point of S_i. Following Definition 4.2.1 we denote the local coordinates of the nodal-point z_i by (x_i, y_i). Let $h = (x_i - x_{i-1})/2$ and $G(x) = \{1 + (F'(x))^2\}^{1/2}$. Then the above integral can be estimated as follows:

$$\left| \int_{S_i} \{f(z) - f(\zeta_i)\} dS_z \right| = \left| \int_{\xi-h}^{\xi+h} \{\hat{f}(x) - \hat{f}(\xi)\} G(x) dx \right| \leq$$

$$\leq \left| \int_{\xi-h}^{\xi+h} \{\hat{f}(x) - \hat{f}(\xi)\}\{G(x) - G(\xi)\} dx \right| + \left| \int_{\xi-h}^{\xi+h} (x-\xi)\hat{f}'(\xi) G(\xi) dx \right| +$$

$$+ \left| \int_{\xi-h}^{\xi+h} (x-\xi) G(\xi) \int_0^1 \{\hat{f}'(\xi + (x-\xi)t) - \hat{f}'(\xi)\} dt\, dx \right| .$$

The first part is less than $Ch_N^3 \|f\|_{1,\alpha}$ and the second part is equal to zero. We proceed to estimate the third part. Let $x - \xi = v$. Since G is bounded it follows that

$$I_3 \le C \left| \int_{-h}^{h} v \int_0^1 \{\hat{f}'(\xi + vt) - \hat{f}'(\xi)\}dt\, dv \right| \le$$

$$\le C \int_{-h}^{h} |v| \int_0^1 |\hat{f}'(\xi + vt) - \hat{f}'(\xi)|dt\, dv \le$$

$$\le C' \int_0^h |v|^{1+\alpha} \|f\|_{1,\alpha}\, dv \le C_2 h_N^{2+\alpha} \|f\|_{1,\alpha}. \qquad \square$$

In the following theorem we discuss the convergence of the approximate solutions $\mu_N \in X_N$ and $\tilde{\mu}_N \in H^{1,\alpha}(S)$ to the exact solution μ. We give error estimates for $\|\mu-\mu_N\|_\infty$, $\|T_N\mu-\mu_N\|_\infty$ and $\|\mu-\tilde{\mu}_N\|_\infty$.

THEOREM 4.2.5 (Approximation theorem). *Let the boundary* $S \in L^{2,\alpha}$; *then for* $N \to \infty$:

(i) $\|\mu-\mu_N\|_\infty \le C_3 h_N \|\mu\|_{1,\alpha}$, *where* μ *is the solution of* (4.2.2) *and* μ_N *of* (4.2.8);

(ii) $\|K(I - T_N)f\|_\infty \le C_4 h_N^{1+\alpha} \|f\|_{1,\alpha}$, *for all* $f \in H^{1,\alpha}(S)$;

(iii) $\|T_N\mu - \mu_N\|_\infty \le C_5 h_N^{1+\alpha} \|\mu\|_{1,\alpha}$;

(iv) $\|\mu - \tilde{\mu}_N\|_\infty \le C_6 h_N^{1+\alpha} \|\mu\|_{1,\alpha}$.

PROOF. (i) From (4.2.2) and (4.2.8) we get:

$$(I - T_N K)(\mu - \mu_N) = \mu - T_N K\mu - 2T_N a = \mu - T_N \mu.$$

Use Lemmas 4.2.3 and 4.2.2 to obtain:

$$\|\mu-\mu_N\|_\infty \le C_1 \|\mu - T_N\mu\|_\infty \le C_3 h_N \|\mu\|_{1,\alpha}.$$

(ii) From the construction of $T_N f$ it follows that

$$K(I - T_N)f(\zeta) = -\frac{1}{\pi} \sum_{i=1}^{N} \int_{S_i} \{f(z) - f(\zeta_i)\} \frac{\cos(n_z, z-\zeta)}{|z-\zeta|}\, dS_z.$$

Let $\zeta \in S_i$. Taking into account Remark 4.1.1, we estimate the (i)-th part of the above sum by:

$$\left| \int_{S_i} \{f(z) - f(\zeta_i)\} \frac{\cos(n_z, z-\zeta)}{|z-\zeta|}\, dS_z \right| \le$$

$$\le C \int_{S_i} |f(z) - f(\zeta_i)|dS_z \le C' \int_{\xi-h}^{\xi+h} |x| \|f\|_{1,\alpha}\, dx \le C'' h_N^2 \|f\|_{1,\alpha},$$

where ξ, h and x are defined in the proof of Lemma 4.2.4. In the other parts of the above sum $z \notin S_i$. We replace z by local coordinates (x,y) and we again use Definition 4.1.3. Since $S \in L^{2,\alpha}$ the kernel-function $\cos(n_z, z-\zeta)/|z-\zeta|$ has a Hölder continuous derivative with respect to x. Hence this function can be written as a series expansion involving powers of $(x-\xi)$. Applying Lemma 4.2.4 we obtain

$$\| K(I - T_N)f\|_\infty \le C'' h_N^2 \| f\|_{1,\alpha} + (N-1)C_2 h_N^{2+\alpha} \| f\|_{1,\alpha} \le C_4 h_N^{1+\alpha} \| f\|_{1,\alpha}.$$

(iii) From equation (4.2.2) we get

$$(I - T_N K)T_N \mu = 2T_N a + T_N K(\mu - T_N \mu)$$

and subtract (4.2.8) to obtain

$$(I - T_N K)(T_N \mu - \mu_N) = T_N K(\mu - T_N \mu).$$

Applying Lemmas 4.2.3 and 4.2.1 we have

$$\| T_N \mu - \mu_N \|_\infty \le C\| K(\mu - T_N \mu)\|_\infty .$$

Since $\mu \in H^{1,\alpha}(S)$, (iii) follows from part (ii) of this theorem.

(iv) From (4.2.2) and (4.2.9) it follows that

$$\| \mu - \tilde{\mu}_N \|_\infty = \| K(\mu - \mu_N)\|_\infty \le \| K(\mu - T_N \mu)\|_\infty + \| K(T_N \mu - \mu_N)\|_\infty .$$

Using parts (ii) and (iii) we obtain the proof of (iv). □

With respect to the smoothness of the boundary S, part (ii) of Theorem 4.2.5 is a modification of results given by KANTOROWITSCH [12, p.127]. He has proven the following: let the boundary S be given by the parametric equations

$$z(t) = X(t) + iY(t), \qquad t \in [0,1],$$

and let $\omega(s,t) = \arg(z(s) - z(t))$. If ω is three times continuously differentiable with respect to s (this assumption is stronger than $S \in L^{2,\alpha}$!) and the function f is two times continuously differentiable (i.e. $f \in C^{(2)}[0,1]$), then

$$\| K(I - T_N) f \|_\infty \le C h_N^2 \| f \|_2,$$

where $\|\cdot\|_2$ is the usual norm of the space $C^{(2)}[0,1]$.

Usually part (iii) of Theorem 4.2.5 is called *super-convergence on the collocation points*. Performing a single iteration of type (4.2.9), the order of super-convergence is extended to all points of the boundary as has been shown by part (iv).

Assuming the boundary to be convex we are able to estimate the error between the exact solution and the approximation (4.2.6). In Theorem 4.2.6 we show how this error depends on the mesh-size h_N.

THEOREM 4.2.6. *Let* $S \in L^{2,\alpha}$ *and let* S *be convex; then for* $N \to \infty$*:*

$$|\phi_d(\zeta) - \hat{\phi}_d(\zeta)| \le C_7\, h_N^{1+\alpha} \|\mu\|_{1,\alpha}, \qquad \textit{for } \zeta \in D,$$

where D *is the interior of* S.

PROOF. Let

$$\tilde{\phi}_d(\zeta) = \frac{1}{2\pi} \int_S T_N\mu(z) \frac{\cos(n_z, z-\zeta)}{|z-\zeta|}\, dS_z,$$

with $\zeta \in D$. For a fixed point $\zeta \in D$ we have

$$|\phi_d(\zeta) - \hat{\phi}_d(\zeta)| \le |\phi_d(\zeta) - \tilde{\phi}_d(\zeta)| + |\tilde{\phi}_d(\zeta) - \hat{\phi}_d(\zeta)| \le$$

$$\le \frac{1}{2\pi} \left| \sum_{i=1}^{N} \int_{S_i} \{\mu(z) - \mu(\zeta_i)\} \frac{\cos(n_z, z-\zeta)}{|z-\zeta|}\, dS_z \right| +$$

$$+ \frac{1}{2\pi} \| T_N\mu - \mu_N \|_\infty \int_S \frac{|\cos(n_z, z-\zeta)|}{|z-\zeta|}\, dS_z.$$

By the same arguments as used for the proof of Theorem 4.2.5(ii) we obtain that the first term is less than $C h_N^{1+\alpha} \|\mu\|_{1,\alpha}$, because $\zeta \notin S$. The second term has been obtained by applying Hölder's inequality. For a convex contour $\cos(n_z, z-\zeta) \ge 0$ for all $\zeta \in D$. We note that

$$\frac{\cos(n_z, z-\zeta)}{|z-\zeta|}\, dS_z = d\theta,$$

where $d\theta$ is the angle formed by two infinitely close radius vectors drawn from the point ζ to the extremities of an arc dS_z. Hence, the integral in the second term becomes $\int_0^{2\pi} d\theta = 2\pi$. By means of part (iii) of Theorem 4.2.5 the second term is also less than $Ch_N^{1+\alpha}\|\mu\|_{1,\alpha}$. □

In aerodynamics one is interested in the tangential velocity, being the derivative of μ. In the following theorem we estimate $\|D\mu - D\tilde{\mu}_N\|_\infty$.

<u>THEOREM 4.2.7</u> (Approximation theorem for the derivative of μ).
Let $S \in L^{2,\alpha}$*; then for* $N \to \infty$*:*

$$\|D\mu - D\tilde{\mu}_N\|_\infty \le Ch_N^{1+\alpha}\|\mu\|_{1,\alpha}.$$

<u>PROOF</u>. From (4.2.2) and (4.2.9) it follows that

$$\|D\mu - D\tilde{\mu}_N\|_\infty = \|DK\mu - DK\mu_N\|_\infty \le$$

$$\le \|DK(\mu - T_N\mu)\|_\infty + \|DK(T_N\mu - \mu_N)\|_\infty.$$

We use Corollary 4.1.3 and Theorem 4.2.5(iii) to prove that

$$\|DK(T_N\mu - \mu_N)\|_\infty \le \|D\|_{H^{1,\alpha}(S)\to R(S)} \|K\|_{R(S)\to H^{1,\alpha}(S)} \|T_N\mu - \mu_N\|_\infty \le$$

$$\le Ch_N^{1+\alpha}\|\mu\|_{1,\alpha}.$$

In order to prove that $\|DK(\mu - T_N\mu)\|_\infty \le Ch_N^{1+\alpha}\|\mu\|_{1,\alpha}$ we follow the lines of the proof of Theorem 4.2.5(ii). From the definition of $T_N\mu$ it follows that

$$DK(\mu - T_N\mu)(\zeta) = -\frac{1}{\pi}\sum_{i=1}^{N}\int_{S_i}\{\mu(z) - \mu(\zeta_i)\}D_\zeta \frac{\cos(n_z, z-\zeta)}{|z-\zeta|}\, dS_z.$$

Let $\zeta \in S_i$. For the (i)-th part of the above sum we obtain

$$\int_{x_i-h}^{x_i+h} \{\hat{\mu}(x) - \hat{\mu}(x_i)\}\frac{\partial R}{\partial \xi}(\xi, x)\,dx \equiv I_i,$$

where $z = (x,F(x))$, $\zeta_i = (x_i,F(x_i))$ and $\zeta = (\xi,F(\xi))$. The function $R(\xi,x)$ is given by (4.1.8). From (4.1.9) it follows that

$$|I_i| \le |\hat{\mu}(x)-\hat{\mu}(x_i)| \int_{x_i-h}^{x_i+h} \left|\frac{\partial R}{\partial \xi}\right| dx \le Ch_N^{1+\alpha} \|\mu\|_{1,\alpha}.$$

In the other parts of the above sum $z \notin S_i$. Replacing z by local coordinates (x,y) and using Definition 4.1.3 we obtain a kernel-function

$$D_\zeta \cos(n_z, z-\zeta)/|z-\zeta|,$$

of which the derivative with respect to x is Hölder continuous with exponent α. The rest of the proof is the same as the proof of Theorem 4.2.5(ii). □

So far we did not say anything about how to solve equation (4.2.8). When the dimension of X_N is small it can be solved by a direct method (e.g. Gaussian elimination). However, when the dimension is large one usually uses iterative techniques. In Section 4.3 we apply multiple grid iterative processes to (4.2.8).

4.3. MULTIPLE GRID METHODS

In this section we apply two multiple grid methods to equation (4.2.8). The first one has been presented in Chapter 2 and is described by approximate inverse $\tilde{B}_p^{(3)}$ and the defect correction process (2.4.2). In this section it is shown that its reduction factor is less than Ch, where h is a measure of the mesh-size. This multiple grid process is characterized by one Jacobi-iteration followed by γ coarse grid corrections. In the second multiple grid process presented in this section another Jacobi-iteration is applied after the coarse grid corrections. It turns out that the reduction factor of this process is less than $Ch^{1+\alpha}$, where α measures the smoothness of the boundary S $(0 < \alpha < 1)$. We need the following assumption for the partition of the boundary.

<u>ASSUMPTION 4.3.1</u>. *The nodal-points* z_i, $i = 0,1,\ldots,N$, *on the boundary* $S \in L^{2,\alpha}$ *are asymptotically uniformly distributed, i.e.*

$$|z_i - z_{i-1}| = h_N(1 + \mathcal{O}(h_N^\alpha)) \quad \textit{for } h_N \to 0,$$

where $h_N = \max_{1\le i\le N} |z_i - z_{i-1}|$.

Let X_p be a short notation for the space X_{N_p} of piecewise constant functions on S. We introduce a sequence of spaces $\{X_p \mid p = 0,1,\ldots\}$ with $N_p = N_0 * 2^p$ such that

$$X_0 \subset X_1 \subset \ldots \subset X_p \subset \ldots \subset R(S).$$

The Banach space R(S) was defined in Definition 4.2.2. The corresponding interpolatory projection operators $T_p : R(S) \to X_p$ are given by (4.2.7) and the corresponding mesh-sizes are denoted by h_p. As a consequence of the above choice of $\{X_p\}$ the following lemma is trivial.

<u>LEMMA 4.3.1</u>. *Let* $q \le p$; *then* $T_p T_q = T_q$.

From now on the operator norm $\|\cdot\|$ is used for operators of which both the domain and the range is the space R(S). Hence

$$\|A\| = \|A\|_{R(S) \to R(S)}.$$

Using the proof of Lemma 4.2.1 we can easily verify that

$$(4.3.1) \qquad \|T_p\| = 1.$$

<u>LEMMA 4.3.2</u>. *Let* X_p *be sufficiently large (i.e.* h_p *sufficiently small) and let* $S \in L^{2,\alpha}$; *then for* $h_p \to 0$:

(i) $\|(I-T_p)K\| \le C_8\, h_p$,

(ii) $\|K(I-T_p)K\| \le C_9\, h_p^{1+\alpha}$,

(iii) $\|T_{p-1}(I-T_p)K\| \le C_{10} h_p^{1+\alpha}$.

<u>PROOF</u>. Let $\Psi = \{Kf \mid f \in R(S) \text{ and } \|f\|_\infty < 1\}$. By Corollary 4.1.3 it follows that $\Psi \subseteq H^{1,\alpha}(S)$. The proofs of parts (i) and (ii) follow from Lemma 4.2.2 and Theorem 4.2.5(ii).

(iii) Let $\zeta_i^{(p-1)}$ be the i-th collocation point on level p-1. The closest collocation points on level p are $\zeta_{2i-1}^{(p)}$ and $\zeta_{2i}^{(p)}$.

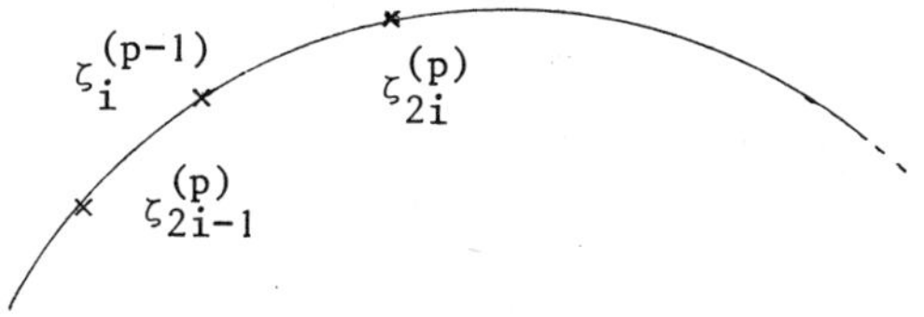

Let $q = p-1$.

$$\|T_q(I-T_p)K\|_{B(S)\to B(S)} = \sup_{f\in\Psi} \|T_q(I-T_p)f\|_\infty =$$

$$= \sup_{f\in\Psi} \max_{1\le i\le N_q} |f(\zeta_i^{(q)}) - \tfrac{1}{2}\{f(\zeta_{2i-1}^{(p)}) + f(\zeta_{2i}^{(p)})\}|.$$

Let (x,y) be a local coordinate system about $\zeta_i^{(q)}$. The coordinates of $\zeta_{2i}^{(p)}$ are (x_{2i},y_{2i}). Using Definition 4.2.2 we obtain for the i-th segment

$$|f(\zeta_i^{(q)}) - \tfrac{1}{2}\{f(\zeta_{2i-1}^{(p)}) + f(\zeta_{2i}^{(p)})\}| = |\hat{f}(0) - \tfrac{1}{2}\{\hat{f}(x_{2i-1}) + \hat{f}(x_{2i})\}|.$$

Since $\hat{f} \in C^{2,\alpha}(D_{\varepsilon,\zeta_i^{(q)}})$ we have

$$\hat{f}(x_{2i}) = \hat{f}(0) + x_{2i}\hat{f}'(0) + O(x_{2i}^{1+\alpha}).$$

The nodal-points are asymptotically uniformly distributed. Since the collocation points are the mid-points it follows that

$$x_{2i} + x_{2i-1} = O(h_p^{1+\alpha}) \quad \text{for } h_p \to 0.$$

Hence

$$|\hat{f}(0) - \tfrac{1}{2}\{\hat{f}(x_{2i-1}) + \hat{f}(x_{2i})\}| = O(h_p^{1+\alpha}) \quad \text{for } h_p \to 0. \qquad \square$$

We once again remark that it is not necessary to approximate the integral operator (see Remark 4.2.1). In order to quote the theorems of Chapter 2 it is obvious to define

(4.3.2) $\quad K_p = KT_p.$

Note that $K\mu_p = K_p\mu_p$ if $\mu_p \in X_p$. From (4.3.1) and parts (i) and (ii) of Lemma 4.3.2 we obtain the following estimates for a_p and b_p, which are defined in Lemmas 2.2.2 and 2.2.5, respectively:

$$a_p \le Ch_p^{1+\alpha},$$

$$b_p \le Ch_p.$$

Hence, the reduction factors of the multiple grid processes of Chapter 2 are less than Ch_p. For the application studied in Section 4.4 $\|K\| \approx 1$ and therefore $\tilde{B}_p^{(4)}$ is not applied in this section.

The reduction factor of $O(h_p)$ is due to the choice of the projection operator T_p. A multiple grid process with a reduction factor of $O(h_p^{1+\alpha})$ can be obtained by performing another Jacobi-iteration after the coarse grid corrections have been applied. This process is described by the approximate inverse $\tilde{B}_p^{(6)}$, which is defined below. The reduction factor of this multiple grid process is related to the two-level algorithm defined by $\tilde{B}_p^{(5)}$ and the defect correction process (2.4.2).

$$\tilde{B}_p^{(5)} = I + T_pK_p + T_pK_{p-1}\tilde{A}_{p-1}^{-1}T_{p-1}T_pK_p,$$

$$\begin{cases} \tilde{B}_0^{(6)} = \tilde{A}_0^{-1}T_0, \\ \tilde{B}_p^{(6)} = I + T_pK_p + T_pK_{p-1}\tilde{Q}_{p-1}^{(6)}T_{p-1}T_pK_p, \quad p = 1,2,\ldots, \end{cases}$$

with $\tilde{A}_p$ and $\tilde{Q}_p$ just as in Section 2.4. In order to estimate the reduction factors we first prove the following lemma.

<u>LEMMA 4.3.3</u>. *Let the finite-dimensional space* X_p *be sufficiently large and let* $S \in L^{2,\alpha}$. *Then for all* $f \in R(S)$:

(i) $(I-K_p)^{-1}f = \{I + K_p(I-T_pK_p)^{-1}T_p\}f$;

(ii) $T_p(I-K_p)^{-1}f = (I-T_pK_p)^{-1}T_pf$.

<u>PROOF</u>. (i) By Lemma 2.2.4 $(I-T_pK_p)^{-1}$ exists on $R(S)$. Let $g = \{I + K_p(I-T_pK_p)^{-1}T_p\}f$. We prove that $g = (I-K_p)^{-1}f$. Indeed, remembering that $K_p = KT_p$,

$$\begin{aligned}(I-K_p)g &= (I-KT_p)\{I + K_p(I-T_pK_p)^{-1}T_p\}f = \\ &= (I-KT_p)f + (I-KT_p)K_p(I-T_pK_p)^{-1}T_pf = \\ &= f - KT_pf + KT_pf = f,\end{aligned}$$

or

$$g = (I-K_p)^{-1}f.$$

(ii) Let $g = (I-K_p)^{-1}f$. From part (i) it follows that

$$T_pg = \{T_p + T_pK_p(I-T_pK_p)^{-1}T_p\}f =$$

$$= \{I + T_pK_p(I-T_pK_p)^{-1}\}T_pf =$$

$$= (I-T_pK_p)^{-1}T_pf. \qquad \square$$

The approximate inverse $\tilde{B}_p^{(5)}$ can be rewritten as follows. From Lemma 4.3.3 it follows directly that

$$(4.3.3) \qquad \tilde{B}_p^{(5)} = I + T_p(I-K_{p-1})^{-1}\, T_pK_p.$$

The reduction factor $\eta_p^{(j)}$, j = 5,6, is defined as in Section 2.4.

THEOREM 4.3.4. *Let* X_p *be sufficiently large and let* $S \in L^{2,\alpha}$*; then for* $p \to \infty$*:*

$$\eta_p^{(5)} \le Ch_p^{1+\alpha},$$

for some constant C.

PROOF. In this proof the following relations are frequently used:

$$\tilde{A}_p = I - T_pK_p \qquad \text{(definition)}$$

and

$$T_pT_{p-1} = T_{p-1} \qquad \text{(Lemma 4.3.1)}.$$

Let $M_p^{(5)} = I - \tilde{B}_p^{(5)}\tilde{A}_p$. We use (4.3.3) to obtain (with $\ell = p-1$):

$$M_p^{(5)} = I - \{I + T_p(I-K_\ell)^{-1}T_pK_p\}\tilde{A}_p =$$

$$(4.3.4) \qquad = T_p[I - (I-K_\ell)^{-1}T_p\tilde{A}_p]K_p =$$

$$= T_p(I-K_\ell)^{-1}[I-K_\ell-T_p\tilde{A}_p]K_p.$$

Since $K_p = KT_p$ it follows that

$$M_p^{(5)} = T_pM_p^{(5)} = M_p^{(5)}T_p.$$

By Lemma 4.3.3(i) it follows that

$$M_p^{(5)} = T_p(K_p-K_\ell)K_p + T_pK_\ell\tilde{A}_\ell^{-1}T_\ell[I-K_\ell-T_p\tilde{A}_p]K_p.$$

Using (4.3.1) - (4.3.2) we obtain that

$$\eta_p^{(5)} \le \|(K_p-K_\ell)K\| + \|K\|\|\tilde{A}_\ell^{-1}\|\|T_\ell(I-K_\ell-T_p\tilde{A}_p)K\|.$$

The first term is less than $\|K(I-T_\ell)K\| + \|K(I-T_p)K\|$. Using Lemma 4.3.2(ii) we obtain the estimate $C_9(h_\ell^{1+\alpha} + h_p^{1+\alpha})$. We proceed to estimate the second term. By Corollary 4.1.3 and Lemma 2.2.4 $\|K\|$ and $\|\tilde{A}_\ell^{-1}\|$ are bounded. There remains to estimate

$$\|T_\ell(I-K_\ell-T_p(I-K_p))K\| \le \|T_\ell(I-T_p)K\| + \|T_\ell(KT_\ell-T_pKT_p)K\|.$$

By Lemma 4.3.2(iii) $\|T_\ell(I-T_p)K\|$ is less than $C_{10}h_p^{1+\alpha}$. Finally we have to estimate

$$\|T_\ell(KT_\ell-T_pKT_p)K\| \le \|T_\ell(I-T_p)KT_\ell K\| + \|T_\ell T_p K(T_\ell-T_p)K\| \le$$

$$\le \|T_\ell(I-T_p)K\|\|K\| + \|K(I-T_\ell)K\| + \|K(I-T_p)K\|.$$

The proof follows from Corollary 4.1.3, Lemma 4.3.2 and Assumption 4.3.1. □

<u>THEOREM 4.3.5</u>. *Let* X_0 *be sufficiently large and let* $S \in L^{2,\alpha}$; *then*

$$\eta_p^{(6)} \le \eta_p^{(5)} + \|K\|\eta_{p-1}^{(6)^\gamma}[\eta_p^{(5)} + \|K\| + Ch_p^{1+\alpha}],$$

for some constant C.

<u>PROOF</u>. From Section 2.4 it follows that $\tilde{Q}_p^{(6)}$ can be formulated as:

$$\tilde{Q}_p^{(6)} = [I - M_p^{(6)^\gamma}]\tilde{A}_p^{-1},$$

where $M_p^{(6)} = I - \tilde{B}_p^{(6)}\tilde{A}_p$. Substitution of this expression into $\tilde{B}_p^{(6)}$ yields

$$\tilde{B}_p^{(6)} = \tilde{B}_p^{(5)} - T_pK_\ell M_\ell^{(6)^\gamma}\tilde{A}_\ell^{-1}T_\ell T_pK_p,$$

with $\ell = p-1$. Hence

$$M_p^{(6)} = M_p^{(5)} + T_pK_\ell M_\ell^{(6)^\gamma}\tilde{A}_\ell^{-1}T_\ell T_pK_p\tilde{A}_p.$$

We now investigate the operator $\tilde{A}_\ell^{-1}T_\ell T_p$. By Lemma 4.3.3 we obtain

$$\tilde{A}_\ell^{-1} T_\ell T_p = T_\ell (I-K_\ell)^{-1} T_p =$$

$$= T_\ell (I-T_p)(I-K_\ell)^{-1} T_p + T_\ell T_p (I-K_\ell)^{-1} T_p =$$

$$= T_\ell (I-T_p)(I+K_\ell \tilde{A}_\ell^{-1} T_\ell) T_p + T_\ell T_p (I-K_\ell)^{-1} T_p =$$

$$= T_\ell (I-T_p) K_\ell \tilde{A}_\ell^{-1} T_\ell T_p + T_\ell T_p (I-K_\ell)^{-1} T_p.$$

Substituting this expression for $\tilde{A}_\ell^{-1} T_\ell T_p$ we proceed to estimate $\eta_p^{(6)}$. Using (4.3.1) - (4.3.2), Lemmas 2.2.4 and 4.3.2 we get

$$\eta_p^{(6)} \le \eta_p^{(5)} + \|K\| \eta_\ell^{(6)^\gamma} \{Ch_p^{1+\alpha} + \|T_p (I-K_\ell)^{-1} T_p K_p \tilde{A}_p\|\}.$$

From (4.3.4) it follows that:

$$T_p (I-K_\ell)^{-1} T_p K_p \tilde{A}_p = T_p K_p - M_p^{(5)}.$$

Hence, the last term between braces is less than $\|K\| + \eta_p^{(5)}$, which completes the proof. □

<u>THEOREM 4.3.6</u>. *Let* X_0 *be sufficiently large, let* $S \in L^{2,\alpha}$ *and let* $\gamma = 2$. *Then*

$$\eta_p^{(6)} \le Ch_p^{1+\alpha}, \quad \textit{for } p \to \infty.$$

<u>PROOF</u>. The multiple grid process is constructed such that $\tilde{B}_1^{(5)} = \tilde{B}_1^{(6)}$. As a consequence $\eta_1^{(5)} = \eta_1^{(6)}$ and by Theorem 4.3.4 $\eta_1^{(5)} \le Ch_1^{1+\alpha}$. Define:

$$v_p = Ch_p^{1+\alpha}, \quad w_1 = v_1$$

and

$$w_p = v_p + w_{p-1}^2 [v_p + \|K\|^2], \quad p > 1.$$

From Lemma 2.3.3 it follows that $w_p \le Cv_p$ if v_1 is sufficiently small, which is the case for h_0 sufficiently small. By induction it is easily verified that $\eta_p^{(6)} \le w_p$. □

We proceed with some remarks about the asymptotic computational complexity. For $N_p \to \infty$ the operation counts (as defined in Section 2.5 by the number of multiplications involved in the matrix * vector computations) per iteration with $\gamma = 2$ are:

$$\tilde{B}_p^{(3)} - 3.5\, N_p^2$$

$$\tilde{B}_p^{(6)} - 4.5\, N_p^2.$$

In this section the operation count of $\tilde{B}_p^{(3)}$ differs from the number given in Section 2.5, because different numerical methods are used (here: piecewise constant functions and collocation at mid-points; Section 2.5: piecewise linear functions and collocation at the end-points of the subintervals). Because of the same reason for both $\tilde{B}_p^{(3)}$ and $\tilde{B}_p^{(6)}$ the number of kernel evaluations is $4/3\, N_p^2$ (Section 2.5: N_p^2), whenever the values are computed once and stored. In our implementation kernel-functions are re-evaluated whenever they are used. In order to compare $\tilde{B}_p^{(3)}$ and $\tilde{B}_p^{(6)}$ we define the asymptotic efficiency by

$$E_p^{(j)} = \eta_p^{\tau_j}, \quad j = 3,6,$$

where $\tau_3 = 1/3.5$ and $\tau_6 = 1/4.5$. By Theorem 4.3.6 we obtain for $\tilde{B}_p^{(3)}$ and $\tilde{B}_p^{(6)}$, respectively:

$$E_p^{(3)} \leq Ch_p^{1/3.5},$$

and

$$E_p^{(6)} \leq Ch_p^{(1+\alpha)/4.5},$$

for $h_p \to 0$. Comparing these efficiencies the multiple grid process defined by $\tilde{B}_p^{(6)}$ becomes the most efficient if $\alpha > 2/7$.

4.4. NUMERICAL RESULTS FOR SMOOTH CONTOURS

In this section we illustrate the theoretical results of the previous sections for the case that the boundary S belongs to the class $L^{2,\alpha}$. We discuss the accuracy of the numerical method of Section 4.2 and we numerically determine the reduction factors of the multiple grid methods described by $\tilde{B}_p^{(3)}$ and $\tilde{B}_p^{(6)}$, which have been studied in the Sections 2.4 and 4.3.

We apply the numerical methods of Section 4.2 to the calculation of non-circulatory, potential flow around a Kármán-Trefftz aerofoil. This aerofoil is obtained by conformal mapping from a circle. The analytical solution is known which enables us to compare the numerical results with the analytical solution.

For potential flow around a two-dimensional body there exists a velocity potential ϕ satisfying Laplace's equation

$$(4.4.1) \qquad \Delta\phi = 0$$

with boundary conditions

$$(4.4.2) \qquad \frac{\partial\phi}{\partial n_e} = 0 \quad \text{along the boundary } S,$$

where $\frac{\partial}{\partial n_e}$ denotes differentiation in the direction of the outward normal to S and, if the flow is non-circulatory:

$$(4.4.3) \qquad \phi(\zeta) \to \mathcal{U}\cdot\zeta \quad \text{for } |\zeta| \to \infty,$$

with $\mathcal{U}$ the velocity vector of the undisturbed flow. In (4.4.3) $\mathcal{U}\cdot\zeta$ denotes the usual inner product in $\mathbb{R}^2$.

We represent the velocity potential ϕ as follows:

$$(4.4.4) \qquad \phi(\zeta) = \phi_d(\zeta) + \mathcal{U}\cdot\zeta,$$

where ϕ_d is defined by (4.1.1) and the doublet distribution μ is such that ϕ satisfies the boundary condition

$$(4.4.5) \qquad \phi^-(\zeta) = 0,$$

or

$$\phi_d^-(\zeta) = -\mathcal{U}\cdot\zeta, \qquad \zeta \in S.$$

This boundary condition yields the following integral equation:

$$(4.4.6) \qquad \mu(\zeta) + \frac{1}{\pi}\int_S \mu(z)\,\frac{\cos(n_z, z-\zeta)}{|z-\zeta|}\,dS_z = -\,2\mathcal{U}\cdot\zeta.$$

It can be verified that $\phi_d^- \in H^{1,\alpha}(S)$ and as a consequence of Corollary 4.1.5 we obtain $\mu \in H^{1,\alpha}(S)$.

<u>LEMMA 4.4.1</u>. *Let* $S \in L^{2,\alpha}$ *and* $\mu \in H^{1,\alpha}(S)$; *then*

$$\frac{\partial\phi}{\partial n_e} = 0 \text{ along } S \Longleftrightarrow \phi^-(\zeta) = 0, \qquad \zeta \in S.$$

PROOF. See MARTENSEN [14, p.247]. □

From this lemma it follows that the solution of the interior Dirichlet problem (4.4.5) also satisfies the Neuman problem (4.4.1) - (4.4.3) for the exterior of the boundary S.

The Kármán-Trefftz aerofoil is obtained from the circle in the χ-plane, $\chi = ce^{i\theta}$, by means of the mapping

$$(4.4.7) \qquad z = F(\chi) = (\chi-\chi_t)^k/(\chi-c(\delta-i\rho))^{k-1},$$

where k measures the trailing edge angle, ρ the camber and δ the thickness of the aerofoil;

$$c = 2\ell(\delta + \sqrt{1-\rho^2})^{k-1}/(2\sqrt{1-\rho^2})^k,$$

$$\chi_t = c(\sqrt{1-\rho^2}-i\rho),$$

with ℓ the length of the aerofoil. To make F single-valued we take the principal value in (4.4.7). In this section we only consider symmetric aerofoils ($\rho = 0$). In Section 4.5 we give numerical results for $\rho \neq 0$. The Kármán-Trefftz aerofoil does not belong to the class $L^{2,\alpha}$ because of the presence of the trailing edge at $z = z_t$. At this point the curvature is not defined. The nice property of the multiple grid methods of a decreasing reduction factor as $N \to \infty$ is completely destroyed. This will be shown in Section 4.5. In this section we remove the corner by the additional mapping

$$(4.4.8) \qquad w = G(z) = z(1-\tilde{z}/z)^{1-1/k},$$

where $\tilde{z}$ is a point inside the aerofoil. By means of (4.4.8) the aerofoil in the z-plane is converted into a quasi-circular shape in the w-plane that certainly belongs to the class $L^{2,\alpha}$, $0 < \alpha < 1$ (see Figure 4.4.1).

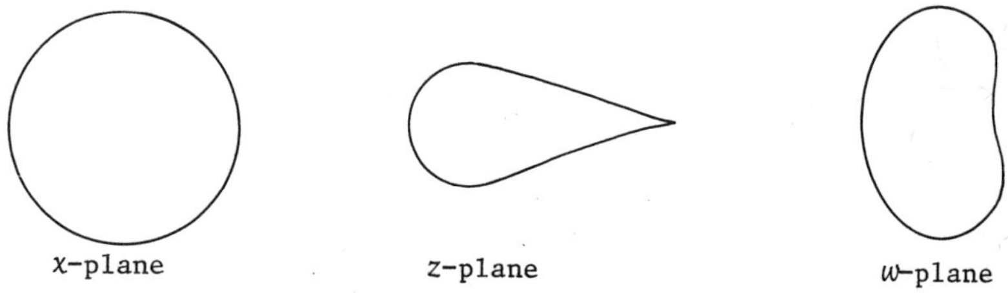

Figure 4.4.1.

Partition of the boundary

We divide the circle in the χ-plane uniformly into N segments. Hence, the nodal-points in this plane are given by

$$\chi_j = ce^{i\theta_j}, \quad \theta_j = 2\pi j/N, \quad j = 0,1,\dots,N.$$

Let $\{\chi_{j-\frac{1}{2}} \mid j = 1,2,\dots,N\}$ be the collocation-points in the χ-plane. Substituting χ_j, $j = 0,1,\dots,N$, into (4.4.7) and (4.4.8), successively, we obtain the nodal-points $\{z_j\}$ in the z-plane and $\{\omega_j\}$ in the ω-plane. The collocation-points in these planes are obtained analogously. Since the mappings (4.4.7) - (4.4.8) are non-linear, the collocation-points chosen in this way are not exactly the mid-points (see Definition 4.2.1), but they are located about in the middle of the segments S_j.

We determine the approximate solution μ_p (dimension N_p) of (4.2.8) by means of the multiple grid iterative processes described by (2.4.2) and the approximate inverses $\tilde{B}_p^{(3)}$ and $\tilde{B}_p^{(6)}$. The algorithm is repeated until the residual is less than 10^{-12}.

The absolute value V_j of the tangential velocity at the point z_j ($z_j \in$ Kármán-Trefftz aerofoil) is obtained numerically by:

$$V_j = \frac{|\mu_{p,j+\frac{1}{2}} - \mu_{p,j-\frac{1}{2}}|}{|\omega_{j+\frac{1}{2}} - \omega_{j-\frac{1}{2}}|} * \left| \left(\frac{d\omega}{dz}\right)\Big|_{z=z_j} \right|.$$

From Theorem 4.2.7 we obtain the following error estimate

$$\text{(4.4.9)} \qquad \max_{1\leq j<N} |V_j - V_{exact}(z_j)| \leq Ch^{1+\alpha}, \quad \text{as } h \to 0,$$

with $V_{exact}(z) = |D\mu(z)|$. In Table 4.1 we give the maximum error in the tangential velocity (i.e. the left-hand side of (4.4.9)) for increasing values of N. Moreover, the total number σ of iterations is given for the iterative methods defined by $\tilde{B}_p^{(3)}$ and $\tilde{B}_p^{(6)}$ with $\gamma = 2$ and $N_0 = 32$.

From this table we conclude that the number of iterations decreases as N increases, which is in agreement with the theory. For the above testcases the error estimate (4.4.9) is found to be satisfactory, since the numerical results suggest that the error is $\mathcal{O}(h^2)$.

In Table 4.4.2 we give the observed reduction factors which are obtained in the same way as in Section 2.5.

k		N = 32	N = 64	N = 128	N = 256
1.90	Error	.12 (-1)	.62 (-2)	.16 (-2)	.39 (-3)
	$\sigma[\tilde{B}_p^{(3)}]$	-	7	5	4
	$\sigma[\tilde{B}_p^{(6)}]$	-	5	4	4
1.99	Error	.53 (-1)	.26 (-1)	.66 (-2)	.19 (-2)
	$\sigma[\tilde{B}_p^{(3)}]$	-	10	6	5
	$\sigma[\tilde{B}^{(6)}]$	-	7	5	4

Table 4.4.1. - Results for flow around a Kármán-Trefftz aerofoil with $\delta = 0.05$, $\ell = 1.0$, $\rho = 0.0$, $\mathcal{U} = (1.0,0.0)$ and $\tilde{z} = (-1.95,0.0)$.

- Error: left-hand side of (4.4.9).
- σ: number of iterations for the multiple grid methods defined by $\tilde{B}_p^{(3)}$ and $\tilde{B}_p^{(6)}$ to obtain a residual less than 10^{-12}.

k	N_0 \ N_p	$\tilde{B}_p^{(3)}$ 8	16	32	$\tilde{B}_p^{(6)}$ 8	16	32
1.90	16	.26			.93 (-1)		
	32	.91 (-1)	.81 (-1)		.27 (-1)	.26 (-1)	
	64	.20 (-1)	.17 (-1)	.16 (-1)	.51 (-2)	.51 (-2)	.48 (-2)
	128	.45 (-2)	.45 (-2)	.45 (-2)	.12 (-2)	.12 (-2)	.12 (-2)
	256	.11 (-2)	.11 (-2)	.11 (-2)	.30 (-3)	.30 (-3)	.30 (-3)
1.99	16	.43			.29		
	32	.26	.24		.14	.15	
	64	.95 (-1)	.11	.86 (-1)	.35 (-1)	.35 (-1)	.29 (-1)
	128	.22 (-1)	.24 (-1)	.20 (-1)	.77 (-2)	.77 (-2)	.77 (-2)
	256	.54 (-2)	.58 (-2)	.50 (-2)	.21 (-2)	.21 (-2)	.21 (-2)

Table 4.4.2. - Reduction factors for the multiple grid methods applied to calculation of flow around a Kármán-Trefftz aerofoil with parameters as in Table 4.4.1.

- Number of coarse grid corrections: $\gamma = 2$.

We recall that the nodal points are asymptotically uniformly distributed. The theory of Section 4.3 predicts the following values for the quotients η_p/η_{p-1}:

$$\tilde{B}_p^{(3)} \; - \; \eta_p/\eta_{p-1} \rightarrow 1/2 \qquad \text{for } N_p \to \infty,$$

$$\tilde{B}_p^{(6)} \; - \; \eta_p/\eta_{p-1} \rightarrow (1/2)^{1+\alpha} \qquad \text{for } N_p \to \infty.$$

Inspecting Table 4.4.2 we conclude that the numerical results of $\tilde{B}_p^{(6)}$ are in agreement with the theory (since $0 < \alpha < 1$), whereas for $\tilde{B}_p^{(3)}$ $\eta_p \to 0$ faster than expected. For $\tilde{B}_p^{(6)}$ the observed reduction factors are smaller than for $\tilde{B}_p^{(3)}$. However, we still have to take into account the operation counts per iteration (see Section 4.3). The efficiency is estimated by:

$$\{\eta(256;32)\}^{\tau_j}, \quad j = 3,6,$$

with $\tau_3 = 1/3.5$ for $\tilde{B}_p^{(3)}$ and $\tau_6 = 1/4.5$ for $\tilde{B}_p^{(6)}$. For convenience of the reader we repeat that $\eta(N_p,N_0)$ is the observed reduction factor with N_p and N_0 the number of segments on the finest and coarsest grid, respectively. From the results given in Table 4.4.2 we obtain the following table:

k	$\tilde{B}_p^{(3)}$	$\tilde{B}_p^{(6)}$
1.90	0.143	0.165
1.99	0.220	0.254

Table 4.4.3. Efficiencies of the multiple grid methods applied to the testcase as specified at Table 4.4.1.

As was already noticed the theoretical estimate for the reduction factor of $\tilde{B}_p^{(3)}$ is pessimistic for the numerical results of Table 4.4.2. That is the reason why for the testcases $\tilde{B}_p^{(3)}$ is more efficient than $\tilde{B}_p^{(6)}$.

Finally, $\tilde{B}_p^{(3)}$ is implemented in our code *solve int eq* (see Chapter 3). Asymptotically for $p \to \infty$, the operation count per iteration is $3.5\,N_p^2$. From condition (3.2.6) it follows that two applications of (2.4.2) with approximate inverse $\tilde{B}_p^{(3)}$ yield an approximation of $\mathcal{O}(h_p)$. In order to obtain an $\mathcal{O}(h_p^{1+\alpha})$ approximate solution in the collocation points (see part (iii) of

Theorem 4.2.5) we have to perform an extra iteration, so that the total amount of work is equal to

$$(4.4.10) \qquad (1 + \tfrac{1}{4} + \tfrac{1}{16} + \ldots)\, 7N_p^2 = 9\tfrac{1}{3}\, N_p^2.$$

The results of *solve int eq* are given in Table 4.4.4, where the predicted error refers to the error in the approximate solution μ_p and *not* to the error in the tangential velocity. Furthermore, we give the final number of coarsest grid intervals (N_0) and finest grid ones (N_ℓ) that *solve int eq* needs to obtain an approximate solution with a desired accuracy of 10^{-4}.

k	Predicted error in μ_p	Actual error in velocity	Final N_0	Final N_ℓ	Final WU
1.90	4.23 (-5)	5.42 (-4)	8	256	8.99
1.95	8.60 (-5)	9.09 (-4)	8	256	8.99
1.99	1.84 (-4)	8.49 (-4)	16	256	8.73

Table 4.4.4. - Results of *solve int eq* applied to the calculation of flow around a Kármán-Trefftz aerofoil with $\delta = 0.05$, $\rho = 0.0$, $\ell = 1.0$, $U = (1.0, 0.0)$ and $\tilde{z} = (-k, 0.0)$.
- Tolerance for *solve int eq*: *tol* $= 10^{-4}$.

From this table we conclude that the number of Work Units is in agreement with the asymptotic amount of work (4.4.10) and that our code *solve int eq* appears to be applicable with respect to this aerodynamic problem.

4.5. APPLICATION OF MULTIPLE GRID METHODS TO THE CALCULATION OF CIRCULATORY FLOW AROUND AN AEROFOIL

The principal aim of this section is to demonstrate the applicability of multiple grid methods to integral equations concerning the calculation of circulatory flow around an aerofoil. In Section 4.5.1 we give an introduction to the problem and we determine the behaviour of the velocity potential near the trailing edge. In Section 4.5.2 we transform the problem into a Fredholm integral equation of the second kind for the doublet distribution μ. Since the aerofoil is not smooth in the sense of Section 4.1 the theory of Sections 4.1 - 4.3 does not hold. Using the results of Section 4.5.1 we determine the regularity of μ. In Section 4.5.3 we discuss a numerical method to compute μ. In aerodynamics this method is called a *first order panel method*. Using a suitable metric we show the convergence of the tangential velocity by means of numerical experiments.

Application of the multiple grid methods of Section 4.3 yields bad results. These methods were based on Jacobi-relaxation. In the present application the Jacobi-relaxation scheme does not smooth the high-frequency errors in the residue. Using another relaxation scheme (paired Jacobi or paired Gauss-Seidel) we obtain a successful multiple grid method.

4.5.1. Introduction

We begin with a discussion of the simple case of flow past the circle of radius a in the complex χ-plane, with a given circulation Γ. The circle is situated in a stream with uniform velocity $U_\infty e^{i\tau}$ far from the circle. The complex potential is known (see BATCHELOR [1]) to be

$$\Omega(\chi) = U_\infty(\chi e^{-i\tau} + \frac{a^2}{\chi} e^{i\tau}) - \frac{\Gamma}{2\pi i} \log \frac{\chi}{a}. \tag{4.5.1}$$

The velocity potential is then

$$\phi(r,\theta) = U_\infty(r + \frac{a^2}{r})\cos(\theta-\tau) - \frac{\Gamma\theta}{2\pi}, \tag{4.5.2}$$

with $r = |\chi|$ and $\theta = \arg \chi$. The flow field is characterized by the parameter $\Gamma/a\, U_\infty$. This is easily seen by noting that the velocity at the circle is

$$\left(\frac{1}{r}\frac{\partial\phi}{\partial\theta}\right)_{r=a} = -2U_\infty \sin(\theta-\tau) - \frac{\Gamma}{2\pi a}.$$

The velocity vanishes at the two points at which

$$\sin(\theta-\tau) = -\frac{\Gamma}{4\pi a U_\infty}.$$

These points are called stagnation points. Let $\chi_t = ae^{i\theta_t}$ to be such a point. In order to make the velocity potential (4.5.2) single-valued we introduce a cut from χ_t to infinity. Along this cut there exists a constant discontinuity in velocity potential as follows from (4.5.2)

$$(4.5.3) \qquad \phi(r,\theta_t+2\pi) - \phi(r,\theta_t) = -\Gamma, \quad \text{for all } r \geq a.$$

The jump in the velocity potential is equal but opposite to the circulation, which is taken positive in clockwise direction.

Once the stagnation point χ_t has been determined, the velocity potential (4.5.2) can be written as

$$(4.5.4) \qquad \phi(r,\theta) = U_\infty(r+\frac{a^2}{r})\cos(\theta-\tau) + 2aU_\infty\theta\ \sin(\theta_t-\tau).$$

At the circle we obtain

$$(4.5.5) \qquad \phi(\theta) = 2aU_\infty\{\cos(\theta-\tau) + \theta\ \sin(\theta_t-\tau)\}.$$

Method of conformal mapping

For many years the method of conformal mapping has been used to generate flow patterns by mapping the region outside the circle in the χ-plane to a region outside an aerofoil in the z-plane through various transformations (e.g. Joukowski and Kármán-Trefftz mappings). Also the inverse way is used in aerodynamics (cf. [10]). In this section we use the method of conformal mapping to deduce known results concerning the behaviour of the velocity potential at the aerofoil near the trailing edge. We first collect some fundamental results of the theory of functions of a complex variable (see CHURCHILL [6]).

For the flow past a circle the complex potential $\Omega(\chi)$ is given by (4.5.1). Let the variable z be related to χ through the relationship

$$(4.5.6) \qquad \chi = F(z),$$

where F is an analytic function of z. Upon the use of (4.5.6), Ω becomes an analytic function of z because the derivative

$$(4.5.7) \qquad \frac{d\Omega}{dz} = \frac{d\Omega}{d\chi}\frac{dF}{dz}$$

exists, due to the existence of the two derivatives on the right-hand side of (4.5.7). After transformation the complex potential can be written as

$$(4.5.8) \qquad \Omega(F(z)) = \phi'(r',\theta') + i\psi'(r',\theta'),$$

with $r' = |z|$ and $\theta' = \arg z$. It follows from the properties of analytic functions that ϕ' and ψ' must satisfy the Cauchy-Riemann conditions and, therefore, the Laplace equation. Since (4.5.1) and (4.5.8) represent the same complex function, we have

$$(4.5.9) \qquad \phi(r,\theta) = \phi'(r',\theta'),$$

apart from some additive constant.

The velocity potential near the trailing edge

An aerofoil in the z-plane can correspond to a circle in the χ-plane only if there is a singular point of the transformation (4.5.6) at the trailing edge ($z = z_t$). Let the external trailing edge angle be equal to $k\pi$, $1 < k \leq 2$. At the point $z = z_t$ the function F in (4.5.6) must transform the trailing edge angle to an angle π at the corresponding point $\chi = \chi_t$ of the χ-plane. Locally (4.5.6) must have the form

$$(4.5.10) \qquad \chi-\chi_t \sim (z-z_t)^{1/k} \quad \text{for } |z-z_t| \to 0.$$

Hence

$$(4.5.11) \qquad |\chi-\chi_t| \sim |z-z_t|^{1/k} \quad \text{for } |z-z_t| \to 0.$$

If χ is a point at the circle we also have

$$(4.5.12) \qquad |\theta-\theta_t| = c|\chi-\chi_t|\{1 + O|\chi-\chi_t|\} \quad \text{for } |\chi-\chi_t| \to 0.$$

The complex conjugate of the velocity follows from

$$(4.5.13) \qquad \frac{d\Omega}{dz} = \frac{d\Omega}{d\chi}\frac{dF}{dz},$$

with $\chi = F(z)$ satisfying (4.5.10). At the trailing edge of the aerofoil $|\frac{dF}{dz}|$ is infinite and so is $|\frac{d\Omega}{dz}|$ unless the circulation is such that $|\frac{d\Omega}{d\chi}|$ goes sufficiently fast to zero at $\chi = \chi_t$. This can be obtained by forcing χ_t to be a stagnation point at the circle. From (4.5.5) we obtain the following expansion for the velocity potential near the stagnation point χ_t:

$$\phi(\theta) = c_1 + c_2(\theta-\theta_t)^2 + O(\theta-\theta_t)^3 \quad \text{for } \theta \to \theta_t.$$

By (4.5.9) a similar expansion must hold for the corresponding points in the z-plane. Using (4.5.11) and (4.5.12) we obtain the following expansion for the velocity potential at the aerofoil near the trailing edge:

$$(4.5.14) \qquad \phi'(|z-z_t|) = \tilde{c}_1 + \tilde{c}_2|z-z_t|^{2/k} + O|z-z_t|^{3/k} \quad \text{for } |z-z_t| \to 0.$$

REMARK 4.5.1. The requirement that x_t is a stagnation point is called the *Kutta condition* (which states that the flow speed must be zero if the exterior trailing edge angle is less than 2π or the speed must be finite if the angle equals 2π).

4.5.2. Calculation of circulatory flow

For circulatory flow one must introduce a cut to make the velocity potential single valued as was shown in the previous section. By the method of conformal mapping it follows (see (4.5.9)) that the velocity potential (4.5.2) also holds for the velocity potential for flow around an aerofoil. However, for the latter case the circulation Γ is *not* known a priori, but follows from the Kutta condition (see Remark 4.5.1). The customary way to satisfy this condition is to construct the cut from the trailing edge to infinity.

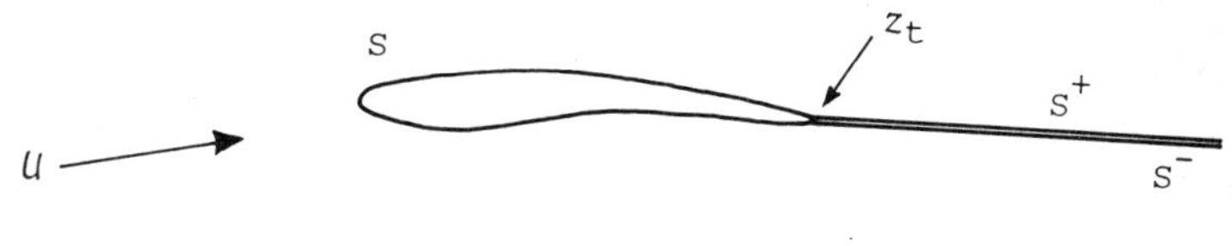

Figure 4.5.1.

We denote the upper and lower side of the cut by S^+ and S^-, respectively. The contour composed of the aerofoil (S) and the cut is denoted by S^-+S+S^+.

From the fundamental results of potential theory (see MUSCHELISCHWILI [15, p.53]) we know that the doublet distribution μ gives rise to a discontinuity in potential

$$(4.5.15) \qquad \phi^+(\zeta) - \phi^-(\zeta) = -\mu(\zeta),$$

provided μ is continuous; if $\mu \in H^{1,\alpha}(S)$ (4.5.15) follows also from Lemma 4.1.1. Along the cut there exists a constant discontinuity in velocity potential which is equal but opposite to the circulation Γ (see (4.5.3)). Since Γ is not known this jump is represented by a constant double layer potential with strength μ^+ and μ^- along S^+ and S^-, respectively. We can represent the velocity potential by

$$\phi(\zeta) = U\cdot\zeta + \frac{1}{2\pi} \int_{S^-+S+S^+} \mu(z) \frac{\cos(n_z, z-\zeta)}{|z-\zeta|} dS_z,$$

or

$$(4.5.16) \qquad \phi(\zeta) = U\cdot\zeta + \phi_d(\zeta) + \frac{1}{2\pi}(\mu^+ - \mu^-)\arg(z_t-\zeta),$$

where ϕ_d is defined by (4.1.1). In this section we denote by $\arg(z)$ with $z \in \mathbb{R}^2$ the real value of the usual function defined by the complex number corresponding to z. The doublet strength along S follows from the boundary condition

$$(4.5.17) \qquad \phi^-(\zeta) = 0 \quad \text{for } \zeta \in S.$$

So far we did not say anything about μ^+ and μ^-, but we still have to satisfy the Kutta-condition. In this thesis we only consider aerofoils with finite trailing edge angle ($1 < k < 2$). For these cases the Kutta condition states that the flow speed must be zero at both sides of the trailing edge. Let ζ^+ and ζ^- be points at the upper and lower part of the trailing edge. The Kutta condition is satisfied if:

$$(4.5.18) \qquad \begin{cases} D\phi^+(\zeta^+) \to 0 & \text{for } |\zeta^+-z_t| \to 0, \\ D\phi^+(\zeta^-) \to 0 & \text{for } |\zeta^--z_t| \to 0, \end{cases}$$

where D denotes differentiation in the tangential direction. These conditions are used to determine μ^+ and μ^-. Using (4.5.15) and (4.5.17) we obtain

$$\phi^+(\zeta) = -\mu(\zeta) \quad \text{for } \zeta \in S.$$

Hence condition (4.5.18) may be replaced by

$$(4.5.19)\quad \begin{cases} D\mu(\zeta^+) \to 0 & \text{for } |\zeta^+ - z_t| \to 0, \\ D\mu(\zeta^-) \to 0 & \text{for } |\zeta^- - z_t| \to 0. \end{cases}$$

Let $r = |\zeta - z_t|$, $\zeta \in S$. The general expansion for the velocity potential at the aerofoil is given by:

$$\phi^+(r) = c_0 + c_1 r^{1/k} + c_2 r^{2/k} + \mathcal{O}(r^{3/k}) \quad \text{for } r \to 0.$$

The constants c_0, c_1 and c_2 need not to be the same at both sides of the aerofoil. The second term induces infinite velocities if the Kutta condition is not satisfied. After condition (4.5.18) has been imposed the term $r^{1/k}$ disappears and the series expansion (4.5.14) also holds for $\phi^+(r)$. From (4.5.15) and (4.5.17) it follows that this expansion must also hold for the doublet distribution. For the upper and lower part of the trailing edge we obtain respectively

$$(4.5.20)\quad \begin{cases} \mu^+(r) = \mu^+ + A^+ r^{2/k} + \mathcal{O}(r^{3/k}), \\ \mu^-(r) = \mu^- + A^- r^{2/k} + \mathcal{O}(r^{3/k}), & \text{for } r \to 0. \end{cases}$$

Since the contour of the aerofoil does not belong to the class $L^{2,\alpha}$ the theorems of the Sections 4.1 - 4.3 are no longer valid. In particular, Theorem 4.1.2 about the regularity of the principal value cannot be proven for the above boundary. To make things worse, we have the following theorem.

THEOREM 4.5.1. *Let μ be essentially bounded on* S. *Then this does not imply* $\bar{\phi}_d \in C(S)$.

PROOF. Let z be a point at the upper part of the trailing edge. We assume that $\arg(z - z_t)$ is constant for $|z - z_t| < \delta$. We call this part of the upper trailing edge Δ.

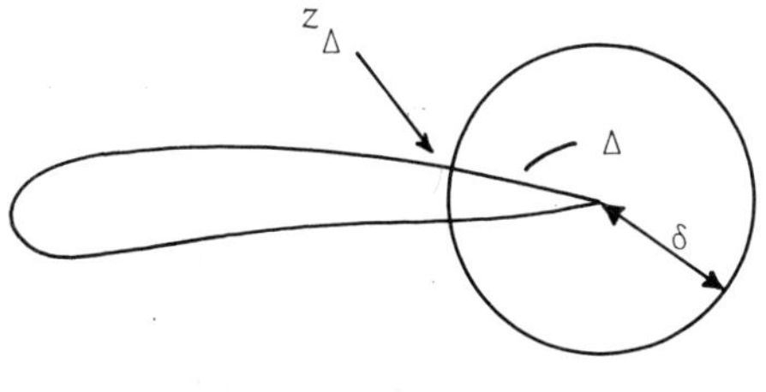

We take the following element of $L_\infty(S)$.

$$\mu(z) = \begin{cases} 1, & z \in \Delta, \\ 0, & z \notin \Delta. \end{cases}$$

Let $\zeta_1 \in \Delta$ and ζ_2 a point at the lower part of the trailing edge. It follows that

$$\bar{\phi}_d(\zeta_1) \equiv 0$$

and

$$\bar{\phi}_d(\zeta_2) = -\frac{1}{2\pi} \arg\left(\frac{z_t-\zeta_2}{z_\Delta-\zeta_2}\right).$$

If $|\zeta_1-\zeta_2| \to 0$ we get

$$\lim_{|\zeta_1-\zeta_2|\to 0} |\bar{\phi}_d(\zeta_1) - \bar{\phi}_d(\zeta_2)| = (k-1)/2.$$

Hence there exists an element of $L_\infty(S)$ for which $\bar{\phi}_d \notin C(S)$. □

As a consequence of this theorem we cannot prove that the operator K as defined by (4.1.15) is a bounded mapping from $L_\infty(S)$ to $C(S)$.

4.5.3. Numerical approach

Application of conditions (4.5.17) and (4.5.19) yields the following integral equation

$$(4.5.21) \qquad (I-K)\mu + \beta(\mu^+-\mu^-) = g,$$

where $\beta(\zeta) = \frac{1}{\pi} \arg(z_t-\zeta)$ and $g(\zeta) = -2\mathcal{U}\cdot\zeta$. The operator K is defined by (4.1.15). As in Section 4.2 we approximate μ by $\mu_N \in X_N$. By means of projection at the collocation points we obtain N equations. However, we have N+2 unknowns $\mu_{N,1} = \mu_{N,2},\ldots,\mu_{N,N}$, μ_N^+ and μ_N^- with $\mu_{N,i} = \mu_N(\zeta_i)$ and $\mu_N^\pm = \mu_N$ $(\zeta;\zeta \in S^\pm)$, so that we need two extra equations. Following (4.5.19) we replace μ_N^+ and μ_N^- by $\mu_{N,N}$ and $\mu_{N,1}$, i.e.

$$(4.5.22) \qquad \begin{cases} \mu_N^+ = \mu_N(\zeta_N), \\ \mu_N^- = \mu_N(\zeta_1), \end{cases}$$

where ζ_1 and ζ_N are collocation points which are closest to the trailing edge at the lower and upper part of S. We have to solve the following equation:

$$(4.5.23)\qquad (I-T_NK)\mu_N + T_N\beta(\mu_{N,N}-\mu_{N,1}) = T_Ng.$$

The principal aim of this section is to show that equation (4.5.23) can be solved efficiently by a multiple grid method. As follows from Theorem 4.5.1 we cannot prove the boundedness of $\|K\|_{L_\infty(S)\to C(S)}$. Problems with respect to the convergence of the iterative process are found to arise in the neighbourhood of the trailing edge. Here the high-frequency errors are not removed by application of K, i.e. by the Jacobi-relaxation, given by:

$$(4.5.24)\qquad \mu_N^{(\nu+1)} = T_Ng + T_NK\mu_N^{(\nu)} - T_N\beta(\mu_{N,N}^{(\nu)} - \mu_{N,1}^{(\nu)}).$$

Inspection of the matrix corresponding to T_NKT_N reveals that the cross-diagonal contains elements of magnitude $1-k + \mathcal{O}(1/N)$ as $N \to \infty$ with k = (exterior trailing edge angle)/π. This occurrence of off-diagonal elements of about the same size as diagonal elements explains why Jacobi-relaxation does not work well. Therefore we apply another relaxation scheme, which we call *paired Gauss-Seidel relaxation*. In order to explain this scheme we first rewrite (4.5.24) as follows:

$$\mu_{N,i}^{(\nu+1)} = g_i + \sum_{\ell=1}^{N} k_{i\ell}\,\mu_{N,\ell}^{(\nu)} - \beta_i(\mu_{N,N}^{(\nu)} - \mu_{N,1}^{(\nu)}) \qquad \text{for } i = 1(1)N.$$

We obtain the *paired Jacobi relaxation* (PJ) by moving the cross-diagonal to the left-hand side:

$$\mu_{N,i}^{(\nu+1)} - k_{ij}\,\mu_{N,j}^{(\nu+1)} = g_i + \sum_{\substack{\ell=1\\ \ell\neq j}}^{N} k_{i\ell}\,\mu_{N,\ell}^{(\nu)} - \beta_i(\mu_{N,N}^{(\nu)} - \mu_{N,1}^{(\nu)}),$$

for $i = 1,2,\dots,N/2$ and $j = N+1-i$. A similar expression is obtained for $i = j$. As a result we have to solve $\frac{1}{2}N$ systems of equations of dimension 2. Substituting the new values of $\mu_{N,i}$ and $\mu_{N,j}$ as soon as they are available we obtain the paired Gauss-Seidel (PGS) relaxation scheme. For $i = 1,2,\dots,N/2$ and $j = N+1-i$ we define

$$\nu_{\ell i} = \begin{cases} \nu & \text{for } i \le \ell \le j, \\ \nu+1 & \text{for } \ell < i \text{ and } \ell > j. \end{cases}$$

We solve simultaneously the following equations:

$$\mu_{N,i}^{(\nu+1)} - k_{ij}\,\mu_{N,j}^{(\nu+1)} = g_i + \sum_{\substack{\ell=1\\ \ell\neq j}}^{N} k_{i\ell}\,\mu_{N,\ell}^{(\nu_{\ell i})} - \beta_i(\mu_{N,N}^{(\bar\nu)} - \mu_{N,1}^{(\bar\nu)})$$

and

$$\mu_{N,j}^{(\nu+1)} - k_{ji}\,\mu_{N,i}^{(\nu+1)} = g_j + \sum_{\substack{\ell=1\\ \ell\neq i}}^{N} k_{j\ell}\,\mu_{N,\ell}^{(\nu_{\ell i})} - \beta_i(\mu_{N,N}^{(\bar\nu)} - \mu_{N,1}^{(\bar\nu)}),$$

for $i = 1,2,\ldots,N/2$ and $j = N+1-i$, with $\bar\nu = \nu$ for $i = 1$ and $\bar\nu = \nu+1$ for $1 < i \le N/2$. The matrix elements k_{ij} can be easily calculated. Let

$$\phi_{ij} = \frac{1}{\pi}\arg\frac{z_j - \zeta_i}{z_{j-1} - \zeta_i}\,.$$

Then

$$k_{ij} = \begin{cases} \phi_{ij} & \text{for } i \neq j,\\[2mm] \phi_{ii} + \begin{cases} 1 & \text{if } \phi_{ii} < 0,\\ -1 & \text{if } \phi_{ii} > 0. \end{cases} \end{cases}$$

The calculations have been performed for several Kármán-Trefftz aerofoils (4.4.7) with thickness-parameter $\delta = 0.05$ and length-parameter $\ell = 1.0$:

I. $k = 1.90$ and $\rho = 0.0$,
II. $k = 1.90$ and $\rho = \sin 0.05$,
III. $k = 1.99$ and $\rho = 0.0$,
IV. $k = 1.99$ and $\rho = \sin 0.05$.

The first and third aerofoil are symmetric; the second and fourth are cambered. The interior trailing edge angle of the testcases I and II is equal to $\pi/10$ and of the cases III and IV it is equal to $\pi/100$.
The velocity U of the undisturbed flow is taken to be $(\cos\tau, \sin\tau)$ with τ the angle of incidence. For the above testcases we give numerical results for $\tau = 0$ and $\tau = \pi/2$.

Using a uniform partition of the circle we obtain the nodal- and collocation-points in the physical z-plane by conformal mapping as in Section 4.4. The successive grids are related by $N_p = 32*2^p$. The approximate solution of (4.5.23) is obtained by the multiple grid method defined in the

ALGOL-68 program given in TEXT 4.5.1:

```
PROC mulgrid = (INT p,σ, VEC u,g) VOID:
IF p = 0
THEN solve directly (u,g)
ELSE TO σ
      DO relax (u,g); INT n = UPB u;
         VEC residue = g-u+K_p*u-β_p*(u[n]-u[1]);
         VEC um := 0_{p-1}, gm := restrict (residue);
         mulgrid (p-1, γ, um, gm);
         u := u + interpolate (um);
         relax (u,g)
      OD
FI
```

TEXT 4.5.1. Multiple grid algorithm.

On level 0 the system of equations is solved by Gaussian elimination. In the above algorithm relaxation is applied both before and after the coarse grid corrections. Therefore, if we take the Jacobi-iteration scheme as *relax*-procedure, we obtain an algorithm that corresponds with the iterative process (2.4.2) defined by $\tilde{B}_p^{(6)}$. Because of reasons of efficiency the number of coarse grid corrections (integer γ) must be less than 4. Here we choose $\gamma = 2$. The interaction between the grids is defined by the procedures *restrict* and *interpolate* which are a representation of the operator T_p, mapping X_{p+1} onto X_p and X_{p-1} onto X_p, respectively. They are specified as follows. Let n be the upper bound of *VEC u*; then:

```
restrict (u) [i]        := 0.5 * (u[2*i-1] + u[2*i]),           i = 1(1)n/2,
interpolate (u) [2 * i] := interpolate (u)[2 * i-1] := u[i],  i = 1(1)n.
```

The aerofoil does not belong to the class $L^{2,\alpha}$ and therefore the estimate for the reduction factor of the multiple grid process using Jacobi-iteration (see Theorem 4.3.6) does not hold. The numerical results confirm that the Jacobi-relaxation scheme is a bad choice for *relax* (see Table 4.5.1). However, the alternative schemes (PJ and PGS) give acceptable reduction factors.

We start our algorithm on level 0 with $N_0 = 32$. The interpolation to level p ($1 \le p \le 3$) of the approximate solution from level p-1 is used as initial guess of the multiple grid process at level p; termination occurs when the residual (in the algorithm below a procedure which computes the maximum of *VEC residue* as defined in *mulgrid*) is less than 10^{-6}. Let *VEC* g_p denote the restriction of g to the collocation points of level p. In ALGOL-68 notation this algorithm reads:

```
solve directly (u0,g0);
FOR p TO 3
DO    up := interpolate (u0);
      TO 25 WHILE residual > 10^-6
      DO mulgrid (p,1,up,gp) OD;
      u0 := COPY up
OD;
```

In the following table we compare the performance of the multiple grid processes using Jacobi-, paired Jacobi- and paired Gauss-Seidel-relaxation. We give the number of iterations to obtain a residual less than 10^{-6}.

Testcase	τ	N = 64 J	N = 64 PJ	N = 64 PGS	N = 128 J	N = 128 PJ	N = 128 PGS	N = 256 J	N = 256 PJ	N = 256 PGS
I	0	15	4	3	13	3	2	11	3	2
	$\pi/2$	15	9	9	4	7	5	2	4	2
II	0	15	8	8	13	5	5	11	3	2
	$\pi/2$	15	10	9	9	7	6	6	4	2
III	0	>25	4	3	>25	3	3	>25	3	2
	$\pi/2$	>25	12	9	19	9	6	9	6	3
IV	0	>25	11	8	>25	7	4	>25	6	4
	$\pi/2$	>25	13	10	>25	10	8	>25	7	3

Table 4.5.1. Number of iterations of the multiple grid process to obtain a residual less than 10^{-6}.

J - Jacobi,

PJ - Paired Jacobi,

PGS - Paired Gauss-Seidel.

From this table we conclude that the multiple grid method using Jacobi-relaxation is not acceptable (it converges too slowly). The process defined by paired Gauss-Seidel relaxation turns out to be the most efficient. In Table 4.5.2 we give its averaged reduction factor that is defined as follows:

$$\hat{r}(\sigma_p) = \left\{ \frac{\| \mu_{p,\sigma_p} - \mu_{p,\sigma_p - 1} \|_\infty}{\| \mu_{p,0} \|_\infty} \right\}^{1/\sigma_p},$$

with $\mu_{p,0} = T_p \mu_{p-1,\sigma_{p-1}}$ and σ_p the number of iterations needed to obtain a residual less than 10^{-6}. As we see from this table the averaged reduction factor is less than 0.4 for all numerical examples, which is quite satisfactory.

Test-case τ		N = 64			N = 128			N = 256			Notes
		σ_1	$\hat{r}(\sigma_1)$	$\hat{r}(\infty)$	σ_2	$\hat{r}(\sigma_2)$	$\hat{r}(\infty)$	σ_3	$\hat{r}(\sigma_3)$	$\hat{r}(\infty)$	
I	0	3	.11 (-1)	-	2	.64 (-2)	-	2	.33 (-2)	-	No lift
	$\pi/2$	9	.33	.57	5	.16	.67	2	.99 (-2)	-	
II	0	8	.29	.57	5	.17	.67	2	.14 (-1)	-	cambered
	$\pi/2$	9	.33	.57	6	.20	.67	2	.88 (-2)	-	aerofoil
III	0	3	.13 (-1)	-	3	.99 (-2)	-	2	.59 (-2)	-	No lift
	$\pi/2$	9	.35	.59	6	.23	.68	3	.56 (-1)	-	
IV	0	8	.29	.59	4	.99 (-1)	-	4	.10	-	cambered
	$\pi/2$	10	.37	.59	8	.30	.68	3	.53 (-1)	-	aerofoil

Table 4.5.2. Numerical results of the multiple grid method with paired Gauss-Seidel relaxation.

σ : number of iterations to obtain a residual less than 10^{-6},

$\hat{r}(\sigma)$: averaged reduction factor,

$\hat{r}(\infty)$: estimate for the spectral radius (-: not available).

Furthermore, we draw the following conclusions:

1. the number of iterations (σ_p) decreases as N increases,
2. on the highest level (N = 256) only few iterations are necessary.

In the following table we discuss the convergence of the numerical solution to the analytical solution. As in Section 4.2 we obtain a continuous numerical solution by:

$$(4.5.25)\qquad \tilde{\mu}_N(\zeta) = g(\zeta) + \beta(\zeta)(\mu_{N,N} - \mu_{N,1}) + K\mu_N(\zeta).$$

The tangential velocities $v(\zeta)$ and $v_N(\zeta)$ are given by the derivatives of the doublet strength:

$$v(\zeta) = D\mu(\zeta), \qquad \text{analytical,}$$

$$v_N(\zeta) = D\tilde{\mu}_N(\zeta), \qquad \text{numerical.}$$

Let S_ε be a small part of the aerofoil consisting of the intersection of S with a disk with radius $\varepsilon > 0$ and centre at z_t. For $\zeta \in S_\varepsilon$ the behaviour of μ is given by (4.5.20), so that the velocity v satisfies

$$v^{\pm}(r) = B^{\pm} r^{\frac{2}{k}-1} + O(r^{\frac{3}{k}-1}), \qquad r = |\zeta - z_t|.$$

Since for practical aerofoils k is close to 2, this behaviour of v causes the numerical approximation to the velocity v_N to converge slowly in the uniform norm $\|\cdot\|_\infty$. In the following we disregard the vicinity of the trailing edge. Suppose that the aerofoil is sufficiently smooth except for a small region near the trailing edge. Taking into account Remark 4.2.2 we obtain a once continuously differentiable numerical solution $v_N(\zeta)$ for $\zeta \in S\backslash S_\varepsilon$ by (4.5.25). By numerical experiments we study the convergence of the tangential velocity in the following metric:

$$\|\mu\|_{\infty,\varepsilon} = \operatorname*{ess\,sup}_{\zeta \in S\backslash S_\varepsilon} |\mu(\zeta)|,$$

with ε chosen as follows. Let $\Pi_N = \{z_0 = z_t, z_1, \ldots, z_N = z_t\}$ and $\chi_N = \{\zeta_1, \ldots, \zeta_N\}$ be the set of nodal-points and collocation-points, respectively. We define ε to be the distance between z_t and the closest nodal-point of Π_{32}, i.e.:

$$\varepsilon = \min(|z_1 - z_t|, |z_{31} - z_t|).$$

The absolute value of the tangential velocity is obtained by pointwise numerical differentiation:

$$|v_N(z_j)| = \frac{|\mu_{N,j+1} - \mu_{N,j}|}{|\zeta_{j+1} - \zeta_j|}, \qquad j = 0, 1, \ldots, N-1,$$

with $z_j \in \Pi_N$ and $\zeta_j \in \chi_N$.

For the testcases I - IV the results are given in Table 4.5.3. For $N > 32$ the results have been obtained by the multiple grid method using paired Jacobi-relaxation. This table suggests that

$$\| v - v_N \|_{\infty,\varepsilon} \leq Ch,$$

where C depends on $\|v\|_\infty$ and the shape of the aerofoil. For some testcases the convergence is somewhat faster; this may be explained by Theorem 4.2.7 The magnitude of $\|v\|_\infty$ explains the size of the errors of testcase IV.

Testcase	τ	$\|\cdot\|_s$ s =	N = 32	N = 64	N = 128	N = 256
I	0	∞	.68 (-2)	.66 (-2)	.63 (-2)	.59 (-2)
		∞,ε	.68 (-2)	.23 (-2)	.35 (-3)	.10 (-3)
	$\pi/2$	∞	.65 (-1)	.23 (-1)	.70 (-2)	.19 (-2)
		∞,ε	.65 (-1)	.23 (-1)	.70 (-2)	.17 (-2)
II	0	∞	.56 (-1)	.16 (-1)	.64 (-2)	.66 (-2)
		∞,ε	.56 (-1)	.16 (-1)	.46 (-2)	.13 (-2)
	$\pi/2$	∞	.72 (-1)	.24 (-1)	.73 (-2)	.21 (-2)
		∞,ε	.72 (-1)	.24 (-1)	.73 (-2)	.18 (-2)
III	0	∞	.12 (-2)	.89 (-3)	.56 (-3)	.36 (-3)
		∞,ε	.12 (-2)	.89 (-3)	.56 (-3)	.30 (-3)
	$\pi/2$	∞	.17	.69 (-1)	.25 (-1)	.83 (-2)
		∞,ε	.17	.69 (-1)	.25 (-1)	.83 (-2)
IV	0	∞	.17 (+1)	.12 (+1)	.64	.31
		∞,ε	.17 (+1)	.12 (+1)	.64	.31
	$\pi/2$	∞	.27	.14	.59 (-1)	.24 (-1)
		∞,ε	.27	.14	.59 (-1)	.24 (-1)

Table 4.5.3. Errors between the numerical and analytical tangential velocity, i.e.
$\|v-v_N\|_\infty$ and $\|v-v_N\|_{\infty,\varepsilon}$

4.5.4. Conclusions and final remarks

The problem of calculation of potential flow around an aerofoil has been formulated as a Fredholm equation of the second kind. Both the collocation method (4.5.23) (to approximate the solution of this equation) and the multiple grid process (to solve the algebraic system of equations) are robust in the sense that no use is made of special transformations and that it can be extended to 3-D problems (see WOLFF [21]). For aerofoils with small interior trailing edge angle the collocation method (4.5.23) has the drawback that many elements (N large) are necessary to obtain a reasonably accurate solution. This leads to a large system of algebraic equations, that may be solved efficiently by a multiple grid method. Asymptotically for $N \to \infty$ only a few multiple grid iterations are necessary.

The use of multiple grid methods is of course not restricted to the collocation method (4.5.23). Using a higher order approximation for the doublet distribution (e.g. cubic splines as used by BOTTA [2]) one can also apply the multiple grid approach. In order to obtain comparable results for a higher order method a coarser partition of the aerofoil suffices then for method (4.5.23). This reduces the dimension (N) of the resulting algebraic system of equations, making the multiple grid method less efficient, but for large values of N it may be applied efficiently. It should be remarked that a higher order approach has the following disadvantages: 1. the cost to generate the algebraic system increases as the order of approximation increases, and 2. the higher order accuracy only occurs if the approach takes into account the singular behaviour of the doublet distribution by means of a special transformation which, in general, affects the robustness of the method. In engineering practice a computational method should be both robust and produce sufficiently accurate results (cf. [19]). Recently SLOOFF [19] has proposed a new technique (i.e. a clustering scheme using coarse grids too) to reduce the work involved in the computation of the matrix corresponding to $T_N K T_N$. By means of this technique the numerical approach (4.5.23) can be made more efficient. Our final conclusion is, that the multiple grid method for integral equations is a promising technique for the computation of potential flow around two- and three-dimensional bodies.

REFERENCES TO CHAPTER 4

[1] BATCHELOR, G.K., *An introduction to fluid dynamics*, Cambridge University Press, 1967.

[2] BOTTA, E.F.F., *Calculation of potential flow around bodies*, Ph.D. Thesis, Rijksuniversiteit Groningen, 1978.

[3] BRAKHAGE, H., *Über die numerische Behandlung von Integralgleichungen nach der Quadratur-formelmethode*, Numerische Mathematik 2 (1960), pp. 183-196.

[4] BREBBIA, C.A., *The boundary element method for engineers*, Pentech Press, London, 1978.

[5] BREBBIA, C.A., *Recent advances in boundary element methods*, Pentech Press, London, 1978.

[6] CHURCHILL, R.V., *Complex variables and applications*, McGraw-Hill, New York, 1960.

[7] DIEUDONNÉ, J., *Foundations of modern analysis*, Academic Press, New York, 1969.

[8] GOLUZIN, G.M., *Geometric theory of foundations of a complex variable*, American Mathematical Society, Providence, Rhode Island, 1969.

[9] GÜNTER, N.M., *Potential theory and its applications to basic problems of mathematical physics*, F. Ungar Pub., New York, 1967.

[10] HALSEY, N.D., *Potential flow analysis of multi-element airfoils using conformal mapping*, AIAA Paper No. 79-0271, 1979.

[11] JASWON, M.A. & G.T. SYMM, *Integral equation methods in potential theory and elastostatics*, Academic Press, London, 1977.

[12] KANTOROWITSCH, L.W. & W.I. KRYLOW, *Näherungsmethoden der höheren Analysis*, VEB Deutscher Verlag der Wissenschaften, Berlin, 1956.

[13] KRASNOSELSKII, M.A. et al., *Integral operators in spaces of summable functions*, Noordhoff International Publishing, Leyden, 1976.

[14] MARTENSEN, E., *Berechnung der Druckverteilung an Gitterprofilen in ebener Potentialströmung mit einer Fredholmschen Integralgleichung*, Arch. Rat. Mech. and Anal. 3, pp. 235-270, 1959.

[15] MUSCHELISCHWILI, N.I., *Singuläre Integralgleichungen*, Akademie-Verlag, Berlin, 1965.

[16] PRENTER, P.M., *A Collocation method for the numerical solution of integral equations*, SIAM J. Numer. Anal. 10 (1973), pp. 570-581.

[17] PRIWALOW, L.L., *Randeigenschaften analytischer Funktionen*, VEB Deutscher Verlag der Wissenschaften, Berlin, 1956.

[18] SLOAN, I.H., NOUSSAIR, E. & B.J. BURN, *Projection methods for equations of the second kind*, Journal of Meth. Anal. and Appl. 69 (1979), pp. 84-103.

[19] SLOOFF, J.W., *Requirements and developments shaping a next generation of integral methods*, Proceedings of IMA Conference on Numerical Methods in Aeronautical Fluid Dynamics, Reading (U.K.), 1981.

[20] STETTER, H.J., *The defect correction principle and discretization methods*, Numerische Mathematik 29 (1978), pp.425-443.

[21] WOLFF, H., *Multigrid method for the calculation of potential flow around 3-D bodies*, Report NW 119, Mathematisch Centrum, Amsterdam, 1982.

[22] ZABREYKO, P.P. et al., *Integral equations - a reference text*, Noordhoff International Publishing, Leyden, 1975.

CHAPTER 5

OSCILLATING DISK FLOW

This chapter deals with the rotating flow due to an infinite disk performing torsional oscillations at an angular velocity $\Omega \sin \omega t$. The study of this type of flow is of considerable importance since it offers the possibility of calculating an "exact" solution to the Navier-Stokes equations. Von Kármán found in 1921 that the equations of motion allowed similarity solutions, in which the radial and tangential velocities vary linearly with radius r, whereas the axial velocity depends only on the distance z to the disk. This chapter is restricted to discussing this category of solutions.

Analytical solutions are found in the literature in the form of series expansions. RILEY [4], BENNEY [1] and ROSENBLAT [5] have developed a solution in the form of a power series in terms of the dimensionless parameter $\varepsilon = \Omega/\omega$. Rosenblat and Benney examined the high-frequency flow ($\varepsilon \ll 1$); Riley also studied the low-frequency case ($\varepsilon \gg 1$).

In this chapter we show that the periodic solution can be obtained by implicit finite difference schemes taking the state of rest as an initial condition. The transient effects are eliminated by calculating a sufficiently large number of periods. In the high-frequency case ($\varepsilon \ll 1$) there is an oscillatory inner layer near the rotating disk. Outside this layer there is a secondary flow which slowly converges to the periodic solution. For $\varepsilon = 0.1$ we have to integrate over 74 periods. In this chapter we reformulate the problem of oscillating disk flow as a non-linear operator equation, that is solved by a multiple grid method. For $\varepsilon = 0.1$ the computational work agrees with the calculation of 7.4 periods of simulation of the physical process. Hence, the amount of work has been reduced by a factor 10. For smaller values of ε the gain of efficiency is even more significant.

The following subjects will be discussed. In Section 5.1 the differential equations and boundary conditions are presented. It is shown that the time-periodic conditions lead to a non-linear operator equation of the second kind. In Section 5.2 we give some results obtained by ROSENBLAT [5] and BENNEY [1]. Moreover, we extend the work done by Benney. Section 5.3 deals with computational methods which are based on ZANDBERGEN's & DIJKSTRA's numerical approach [6]. Numerical results are given in Section 5.4.

The stimulus for the present study came from the interest of Philips Research Laboratories in an industrial application of oscillating disk flow.

5.1. INTRODUCTION

The basic equations for incompressible, viscous flow are the Navier-Stokes and continuity equations. By means of the Von Kármán similarity transformations the velocities (u,v,w) in a cylindrical coordinate system (r,ϕ,z) can be written as:

$$u = \Omega r f(z',t'), \qquad v = \Omega r g(z',t'), \qquad w = -2(2\nu\omega)^{\frac{1}{2}} h(z',t'),$$

where ν is the kinematic viscosity, $z' = (\frac{\Omega^2}{2\nu\omega})^{\frac{1}{2}} z$ and $t' = \omega t$. Substituting these similarity solutions in the Navier-Stokes and continuity equations and omitting the primes, we obtain:

$$(5.1.1) \qquad \begin{cases} \frac{\omega}{\Omega} f_t = \frac{\Omega}{2\omega} f_{zz} + 2hf_z - f^2 + g^2 - k, \\ \frac{\omega}{\Omega} g_t = \frac{\Omega}{2\omega} g_{zz} + 2hg_z - 2fg, \end{cases}$$

$$(5.1.2) \qquad h_z = f,$$

where k is a measure of the radial pressure gradient. A fourth equation serves to determine the axial pressure gradient after the velocity components have been found. This equation has been omitted.

The boundary conditions are given by the no-slip conditions. Assuming that an infinite disk oscillates in the plane $z = 0$, they are:

$$(5.1.3) \qquad f(0,t) = h(0,t) = 0, \qquad g(0,t) = \sin t.$$

Furthermore, we need conditions at infinity. Assuming that the radial and azimuthal components of the velocity tend to zero (hence, only axial inflow is possible), we get

(5.1.4) $f(z,t) \to 0, \quad g(z,t) \to 0 \quad \text{for } z \to \infty.$

It can be shown that $k(t) = \lim_{z\to\infty} g^2(z,t)$; hence, in our application $k \equiv 0$.

This problem involves two relevant length scales: 1. Von Kármán layer thickness $(\nu/\Omega)^{\frac{1}{2}}$ and 2. the Stokes layer thickness $(\nu/\omega)^{\frac{1}{2}}$. Apparently, the oscillating disk flow is characterized by the parameter $\varepsilon = \Omega/\omega$, which determines the ratio of the Stokes layer thickness to the Von Kármán layer thickness.

In this chapter we discuss two computational methods to find the periodic solution, i.e. the solution that satisfies

(5.1.5) $h(z,0) = h(z,2\pi), \quad g(z,0) = g(z,2\pi).$

The first method is based on simulation of the physical process by taking the state of rest as an initial condition and eliminating the transient effects by integration in time. In mathematical terminology this process can be interpreted as Picard's method for computing a fixed point. Let the velocity vector be:

$$\upsilon = (f,g,h).$$

Denote by $(\upsilon(z,t);\upsilon_0)$ the solution of the usual initial-value problem (5.1.1) - (5.1.4) with initial data:

(5.1.6) $\upsilon(z,0) = \upsilon_0(z).$

Assume that the initial data υ_0 belong to a suitable class L. Define a map of L into itself by the equation

(5.1.7) $K_\varepsilon \upsilon_0 := (\upsilon(\cdot,2\pi);\upsilon_0),$

being the solution of (5.1.1) - (5.1.4) and (5.1.6) at $t = 2\pi$. Since (5.1.1) - (5.1.2) is a parabolic system, K_ε may be expected to have a smoothing influence, just as the integral operators of the Fredholm equations studied in the preceding chapters. In operator notation simulation of the physical process is written as the Picard sequence

(5.1.8) $\upsilon_{i+1} = K_\varepsilon \upsilon_i, \quad \text{with } \upsilon_0 = 0.$

The periodic condition (5.1.5) can be rewritten as

$$(5.1.9) \qquad \nu = K_\varepsilon \nu, \quad \nu \in L.$$

We remark that equation (5.1.9) is a non-linear operator equation of the second kind. For $\varepsilon < 1$ (5.1.8) converges slowly. Therefore, we will devise another method. Since equation (5.1.9) has a superficial resemblance with a Fredholm equation of the second kind, we will try to apply a multiple grid method to (5.1.9).

5.2. ANALYTICAL RESULTS

The oscillating disk problem has been studied by ROSENBLAT [5], BENNEY [1] and RILEY [4]. Rosenblat and Benney have given solutions in the form of asymptotic expansions for the high-frequency case, while Riley considers the low-frequency case too. This section only deals with the high-frequency flow. We give some results of the above papers and extend the work done by Benney.

Rosenblat has shown that the steady part of the radial component of velocity persists outside an inner boundary layer of thickness $O(\nu/\omega)^{\frac{1}{2}}$ to which the azimuthal component of velocity and the unsteady part of the radial component are confined. In particular he shows that the outer boundary layer is of thickness $O(\varepsilon^{-1})$ times the thickness of the inner layer. The basic equations (5.1.1)-(5.1.2) were obtained by means of the dimensionless coordinate

$$(5.2.1) \qquad x' = z/d, \quad d = \varepsilon^{-1}(2\nu/\omega)^{\frac{1}{2}}$$

It is clear that d is a measure for the thickness of the outer Von Kármán layer. To study the inner flow we introduce

$$(5.2.2) \qquad \eta = z'/\varepsilon, \quad G(\eta,t) = g(z',t), \quad H(\eta,t) = \varepsilon^{-1}h(z',t).$$

From now on the primes will be omitted. After substitution we obtain

$$(5.2.3) \qquad \begin{cases} H_{\eta t} = \frac{1}{2}H_{\eta\eta\eta} + \varepsilon(2HH_{\eta\eta} - H_\eta^2 + G^2), \\ \\ G_t = \frac{1}{2}G_{\eta\eta} + 2\varepsilon(HG_\eta - H_\eta G). \end{cases}$$

The boundary conditions for H and G are

$$(5.2.4)\qquad \begin{cases} H = H_\eta = 0, \quad G = \sin(t) \text{ at } \eta = 0, \\ H_\eta \to 0, \quad G \to 0 \quad \text{for } \eta \to \infty. \end{cases}$$

These equations are identical with those of Rosenblat, Benney and Riley. Rosenblat has given a solution of (5.2.3) - (5.2.4) for small ε in the form of the following series expansions:

$$(5.2.5)\qquad H(\eta,t) = \sum_{n=0}^{\infty} \varepsilon^n H_n(\eta,t) \quad \text{and} \quad G(\eta,t) = \sum_{n=0}^{\infty} \varepsilon^n G_n(\eta,t).$$

He shows that $H_0 = G_1 = 0$ and

$$(5.2.6)\qquad G_0(\eta,t) = e^{-\eta} \sin(t-\eta),$$

$$(5.2.7)\qquad H_1(\eta,t) = -\frac{1}{8}(1-2\eta-e^{-2\eta}) + \frac{1}{16}\Big\{(2-\sqrt{2})\cos(2t+\pi/4) + $$
$$+ 2e^{-\sqrt{2}\eta} \cos(2t-\sqrt{2}\eta+\pi/4) - \sqrt{2}\, e^{-2\eta} \cos(2t-2\eta+\pi/4)\Big\}.$$

From (5.2.7) it can be seen that for large values of η the axial velocity increases linearly with η and the radial component of velocity H_η is not zero, so that the boundary condition $H_\eta(\infty) = 0$ is not satisfied. Riley has shown that the series expansions (5.2.5) are suitable for describing an oscillatory inner layer near the rotating disk. Outside this layer there is a secondary flow. Using matched asymptotic expansions Riley was able to find a steady solution representing the first term of an outer expansion. The second time-dependent term can easily be resolved with the multiple scaling technique that Benney used for this problem. He determined series expansions valid uniformly throughout the region of flow. The coefficients in the series expansions (5.2.5) are not only dependent on η and t, but also on $z = \varepsilon\eta$. Benney shows that

$$H(\eta,z,t) = H_0(z) + \varepsilon H_1(\eta,z,t) + \mathcal{O}(\varepsilon^2).$$

It is found that H_0 has to satisfy

$$(5.2.8)\qquad \begin{cases} H_0''' - 2H_0'^2 + 4H_0H_0'' = 0, \\ H_0(0) = 0, \quad H_0'(0) = 1/4, \quad H_0'(\infty) = 0, \end{cases}$$

where the primes denote differentiation with respect to z. In particular, Benney and Riley have calculated:

$$H_0''(0) = -0.207 \quad \text{and} \quad H_0(\infty) = 0.265.$$

Instead of (5.2.7) Benney finds the following solution for $H_1(\eta,z,t)$:

$$H_1(\eta,z,t) = a_0 + a_1e^{-2\eta} + a_2\cos(2t+\pi/4) + a_3e^{-\sqrt{2}\eta}\cos(2t-\sqrt{2}\eta+\pi/4) + a_4e^{-2\eta}\cos(2t-2\eta+\pi/4),$$

where $a_0,\ldots,a_4$ are functions of $z = \varepsilon\eta$ for which Benney derived appropriate differential equations and boundary conditions. For verifying our numerical results we are only interested in $H_1(\infty,t)$. From Benney's paper it is easily seen that $a_2 \equiv \frac{1}{16}(2-\sqrt{2})$ and we extend his work by determining the function a_0, which follows from

$$(5.2.9)\qquad a_0''' + 4H_0a_0'' - 4H_0'a_0' + 4H_0''a_0 = 0$$

and

$$(5.2.10)\qquad a_0(0) = -\frac{1}{8}, \quad a_0'(0) = a_0'(\infty) = 0,$$

where H_0 is equal to the solution of (5.2.8). Two independent solutions of (5.2.9) are

$$a_0^{(1)}(z) = zH_0'(z) + H_0(z) \quad \text{and} \quad a_0^{(2)}(z) = H_0'(z),$$

which may be verified by substitution into (5.2.9) and using (5.2.8). The latter solution decreases exponentially to zero for large values of z. The former solution goes exponentially to the constant value $H_0(\infty)$. A third solution increases linearly if z tends to infinity. This can be seen from the representation of (5.2.9) for large values of z:

$$a_0''' + 4H_0 a_0'' \sim 0 \quad \text{for } z \to \infty.$$

The general solution is a linear combination of these three independent solutions. Taking into account the boundary condition $a_0'(\infty) = 0$, the third solution is not acceptable for our problem. The solution of (5.2.9) - (5.2.10) becomes:

$$a_0(z) = H_0''(0)\{zH_0'(z) + H_0(z)\} - \tfrac{1}{2}H_0'(z).$$

In particular the axial inflow at infinity is found to be:

(5.2.11) $$H(\infty,t) = H_0(\infty) + \varepsilon\{H_0''(0)H_0(\infty) + \frac{1}{16}(2-\sqrt{2})\cos(2t+\pi/4)\} + O(\varepsilon^2).$$

5.3. NUMERICAL APPROACH

This section is divided into two parts: 1. the numerical solution of the initial-boundary value problem (5.1.1) - (5.1.4) with the initial data (5.1.6) and 2. numerical methods for finding periodic solutions satisfying (5.1.9).

5.3.1. Discretization of the initial-boundary value problem

Consider the partial differential equations (5.1.1) - (5.1.2) with the boundary conditions (5.1.3) - (5.1.4) and the initial data (5.1.6). To this problem we apply implicit finite difference techniques in combination with an appropriate stretching function for the construction of the computational grid. In calculations the boundary conditions (5.1.4) are applied at a finite value $z = \ell$:

(5.3.1) $$f(\ell,t) = g(\ell,t) = 0.$$

In Section 5.2 it was shown that the high-frequency flow ($\varepsilon \ll 1$) consists of a Stokes layer near the rotating disk and a secondary outer layer. The azimuthal component of velocity follows from (5.2.5) - (5.2.6):

(5.3.2) $$g(z,t) = e^{-z/\varepsilon}\sin(t - z/\varepsilon) + O(\varepsilon^2) \quad \text{for } \varepsilon \to 0.$$

We want to resolve the flow structure near the disk with a limited number of mesh-points. Taking into account (5.3.2) we transform the z-coordinate by

$$z = \phi(x) \equiv \ell(\varepsilon x + (1-\varepsilon)x^3), \quad x \in [0,1]. \tag{5.3.3}$$

We denote the inverse function of ϕ by ψ. The computational mesh covering the range $0 \le x \le 1$ is chosen uniform with the stepsize $\Delta x = 1/N$. The equations (5.1.1) are integrated in time by means of the Euler-backward formula: at mesh-point $x_j = j\Delta x$ and at the time $t_k = k\Delta t$ ($\Delta t = 2\pi/T$) we approximate f_t by:

$$f_t(x_j,t_k) \approx \frac{f_{j,k} - f_{j,k-1}}{\Delta t}.$$

The first and second order spatial derivatives are discretized by central differences at $t = t_k$. The left- and right-hand sides of (5.1.2) are integrated by means of the mid-point and trapezoidal rule, respectively. In this way we obtain a system of finite difference equations for the quantities $h_{j,k}$, $g_{j,k}$ and $f_{j,k}$. For convenience we introduce:

$$P(x) = \psi_z(z(x)), \quad Q(x) = \psi_{zz}(z(x)).$$

From (5.1.1) - (5.1.2) we thus obtain:

$$P_{j-\frac{1}{2}}(h_{j,k} - h_{j-1,k}) - \frac{\Delta x}{2}(f_{j-1,k} + f_{j,k}) = 0 \quad \text{for } j = 1(1)N, \tag{5.3.4}$$

$$g_{j,k} - g_{j,k-1} - \varepsilon\frac{\Delta t}{\Delta x^2}\Big(\frac{\varepsilon}{2} P_j^2(g_{j+1,k} - 2g_{j,k} + g_{j-1,k}) + \tag{5.3.5}$$
$$+ \frac{\Delta x}{2}(\frac{\varepsilon}{2}Q_j + 2P_jh_{j,k})(g_{j+1,k} - g_{j-1,k}) - 2\Delta x^2 f_{j,k}g_{j,k}\Big) = 0$$
$$\text{for } j = 1(1)N-1,$$

$$f_{j,k} - f_{j,k-1} - \varepsilon\frac{\Delta t}{\Delta x^2}\Big(\frac{\varepsilon}{2}P_j^2(f_{j+1,k} - 2f_{j,k} + f_{j-1,k}) + \tag{5.3.6}$$
$$+ \frac{\Delta x}{2}(\frac{\varepsilon}{2}Q_j + 2P_jh_{j,k})(f_{j+1,k} - f_{j-1,k}) - \Delta x^2 f_{j,k}^2 + \Delta x^2 g_{j,k}^2\Big) = 0$$
$$\text{for } j = 1(1)N-1.$$

A method of solving this system of 3N-2 non-linear algebraic equations by means of Newton iteration has been given by ZANDBERGEN & DIJKSTRA [6]. This approach leads to a linear system of equations for the Newton corrections. The bandwidth of the system is seven and the matrix routine takes advantage of this property. The Newton iterative process is terminated if the residual is less than 10^{-6}.

5.3.2. Numerical methods for computing periodic solutions

Using the above finite difference approach we define the discrete counterpart of the operator K_ε by $K_{\varepsilon;N,T,\ell}$. Let g_k^N be the following grid-function:

$$g_k^N = (g_{0,k}, g_{1,k}, \ldots, g_{N,k});$$

f_k^N and h_k^N are similarly defined.

In discrete operator notation the periodic condition reads:

$$(5.3.7) \qquad \upsilon_N = K_{\varepsilon;N,T,\ell}\, \upsilon_N,$$

where $\upsilon_N = (f_0^N, g_0^N, h_0^N) = (f_T^N, g_T^N, h_T^N)$.

In this section we propose two computational methods to solve (5.3.7): (1) simulation of the physical process by Picard iteration and (2) a multiple grid method, as discussed in Chapter 2. In the first method the parameters ε, N, T and ℓ are fixed. In the second method the parameters N and T are taken from a sequence $\{(N_p, T_p)\}_{p=0,1,\ldots,L}$ such that with $p = L$ we have $N_L = N$, $T_L = T$ and with $p < q \le L$ we have $N_p \le N_q$, $T_p \le T_q$ (i.e. a smaller p corresponds with a coarser discretization).

A. Simulation of the physical process

We take the state of rest ($\upsilon_N^{(0)} \equiv 0$) as an initial condition. The transient effects are eliminated by Picard's method:

$$(5.3.8) \qquad \upsilon_N^{(i+1)} = K_{\varepsilon;N,T,\ell}\, \upsilon_N^{(i)}.$$

The iteration index i counts the number of periods that is calculated. This process is truncated if the residual $\| \upsilon_N^{(i)} - K_{\varepsilon;N,T,\ell} \upsilon_N^{(i)} \|$ is less than $0.5\ 10^{-4}$. Here

$$\| v_N \| = \max_{0\le j\le N} |g_{j,0}| + \max_{0\le j\le N} |h_{j,0}|.$$

B. Multiple grid method

We introduce a sequence of grids with $N_p = 20 * 2^p$ and $T_p = 8 * 2^p$. The integer p is called *level*. We replace the subscript N_p by p:

$$v_{N_p} = v_p \quad \text{and} \quad K_{\varepsilon;N_p,T_p,\ell} = K_{\varepsilon;p}.$$

By $v_p[j]$ we denote the velocity at grid-point x_j on level p:

$$v_p[j] = (f_{j,0}, g_{j,0}, h_{j,0}).$$

The addition $v_p[j] + v_p[k]$ and the multiplication $c * v_p[j]$ are defined as usual (element by element). The interaction between the grids is defined by piecewise linear interpolation:

$$\text{interpolate}(v_p)[j] = \begin{cases} v_p[j/2] & , j = 0,2,\dots,N_p \\ 0.5 * (v_p[\frac{j+1}{2}] + v_p[\frac{j-1}{2}]), & j = 1,3,\dots,2N_p-1, \end{cases}$$

and by injection

$$\text{restrict}(v_p)[j] = v_p[2j], \quad j = 0,1,\dots,\tfrac{1}{2}N_p.$$

We use a multiple grid method, that starts on level 0 with simulation of the physical process (method A). For small values of ε we apply continuation. Suppose we have the following ε-sequence: $\{\varepsilon_\ell \mid \varepsilon_0 > \varepsilon_1 > \dots > \varepsilon_M$ with $\varepsilon_0 = 1\}$. At each stage of this continuation process we approximately solve the equation $v_0 = K_{\varepsilon_\ell;0}\, v_0$ by (5.3.8) until the residual is less than $0.5\ 10^{-3}$. As initial guess for (5.3.8) we take the solution of the previous stage ($\varepsilon = \varepsilon_{\ell-1}$). For $\varepsilon = \varepsilon_0$ we take the state of rest. Denote the solution of this continuation method by $v_0(\varepsilon_0,\varepsilon_1,\dots,\varepsilon_M)$.

Since (5.3.7) is a non-linear equation it is only solved approximately. Let U_p be an approximation to the solution v_p of (5.3.7) on level p. We define the defect of U_p by

$$d_p = U_p - K_{\varepsilon;p} U_p.$$

The multiple grid method is given by the ALGOL-68 program in TEXT 5.3.1, where *VELO* is a mode for the vector of unknowns:

MODE VELO = *STRUCT*(*VEC* f,g,h).

The structure of this multiple grid algorithm has been proposed by HACKBUSCH [3] for the numerical solution of general time-periodic parabolic problems.

On level 0 of *multigrid* we use overrelaxation for extremely small values of ε. The parameter ω_i takes the values 1, 2 and 4. Initially we put $\omega_i = 1$. If the axial inflow converges slowly it is multiplied by a factor 2. As soon as the residual increases the value $\omega_i = 1$ is restored.

```
PROC compute periodic solution = (#to level# INT ℓ) VOID:
(U_0 := v_0(ε_0,ε_1,...,ε_M);
 FOR j TO ℓ
 DO d_{j-1} := U_{j-1} - K_{ε;j-1} U_{j-1};
    U_j := interpolate(U_{j-1});
    multigrid(j,1,U_j,0_j)
 OD
 );

PROC multigrid = (INT m,σ,REF VELO U, VELO y) VOID:
(IF m = 0
 THEN FOR i TO 50 WHILE residual > δ_ε
      DO VELO r = y - U + K_{ε;m} U;
         residual := ‖r‖;
         U := U + ω_i * r
      OD
 ELSE TO σ
      DO U := y + K_{ε;m} U;
         VELO d = d_{m-1}-restrict(y-U+K_{ε;m} U);
         VELO v := COPY U_{m-1};
         multigrid(m-1,2,v,d);
         U := U + interpolate(U_{m-1} - v)
      OD
 FI
);
```

TEXT 5.3.1. Multiple grid algorithm for the computation of periodic solutions of parabolic equations.

5.4. NUMERICAL RESULTS

From ZANDBERGEN & DIJKSTRA [6] it is known that Von Kármán's rotating disk solution can be represented sufficiently accurate with $\ell = 12$, hence we fix infinity at this value. We give numerical results for the following values of ε:

$$\varepsilon_0 = 1, \quad \varepsilon_1 = 0.5, \quad \varepsilon_2 = 0.1, \quad \varepsilon_3 = 0.05.$$

This sequence is also applied in the continuation process that is used to find an approximation $\mathcal{U}_0$ of the multiple grid method, e.g. for $\varepsilon = 0.1$ we have $\mathcal{U}_0 := v_0\ (1, 0.5, 0.1)$. For $N = 160$ and $T = 64$ (i.e. $\Delta x = 1/160$, $\Delta t = \pi/32$), we compare the performances of simulation of the physical process (method A) and the multiple grid method (B). On the coarsest grid the latter method needs 20 stepsizes in space and 8 stepsizes in time; hence it uses four levels: 0,1,2 and 3. The corresponding grids are given by the sequence

$$\{(N_p,T_p)\}_{p=0,1,2,3} = \{(20,8),(40,16),(80,32),(160,64)\}.$$

The numerical results contain the following errors:

(i) iteration error, caused by the above iterative methods A and B,
(ii) cut-off error, arising from the use of (5.3.1) instead of (5.1.4). In our experiments this error is small as compared with:
(iii) discretization errors, introduced by the approximation of (5.1.1) - (5.1.2) by means of (5.3.4) - (5.3.6).

Let a work unit be defined by the computational work needed for calculating one Picard iterate with $N = 160$ and $T = 64$. In the table below we compare the computed axial inflow at infinity (i.e. $h_{N,0}$) with the value of its asymptotic approximation (5.2.11) for $\varepsilon \to 0$. Between parentheses we give the number of work units and the iteration error $\|\mathcal{U}_N - \mathcal{K}_{\varepsilon;N,T,\ell}\, \mathcal{U}_N\|$, where $\mathcal{U}_N$ is the final solution.

On level 0 of the multiple grid method we used Picard iteration (i.e. $\omega_i \equiv 1$) for $\varepsilon \geq 0.1$. The iterative process was terminated when the residual was less than $\delta_\varepsilon = 0.5 \quad 10^{-4}$. For $\varepsilon = 0.05$ we have applied overrelaxation ($1 \leq \omega_i \leq 4$) and we have put $\delta_{0.05} = 10^{-7}$. That is the reason why the computational work increased for this case.

ε	Method A	Method B	(5.2.11)
1.0	0.2014 (8, 4.4 10^{-5})	0.2014 (6.8, 9.3 10^{-7})	0.2360
0.5	0.1177 (17, 4.7 10^{-5})	0.1178 (7.0, 3.9 10^{-6})	0.1253
0.1	0.0236 (74, 4.9 10^{-5})	0.0271 (7.4, 1.6 10^{-5})	0.0262
0.05	0.0083 (72, 4.9 10^{-5})	0.0137 (12.5, 3.3 10^{-6})	0.0132

Table 5.4.1. Axial inflow
(number of work units, residual).

From Table 5.1 we conclude that the multiple grid method becomes more efficient as ε decreases. For $\varepsilon = 0.1$ the computational work has been reduced by a factor 10. For $\varepsilon = 0.1$ and $\varepsilon = 0.05$ the numerical results of method A still contain a low-frequency error. In this case the test for termination of the physical process is not adequate. This process converges slowly, as can be seen From Figure 5.4.1, in which we have displayed the axial inflow as a function of the number of periods. For $\varepsilon = 0.05$ the axial inflow is still increasing after 72 periods. The same phenomenon occurs on the coarsest grid of the multiple grid method. Therefore we have applied overrelaxation.

Figure 5.4.1.

Dependence of the axial inflow on the number of periods.

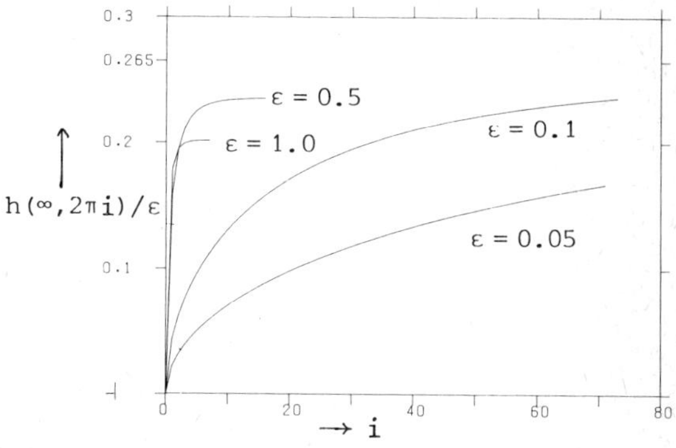

The results of our analysis are given in Figures 5.4.2 - 5.4.3. The profiles of the variables f/ε, g and h/ε are displayed in Figure 5.4.2. We see that there is an oscillatory boundary layer. For smaller values of ε (see Figures 5.4.2(c-d)) the azimuthal component of velocity (g) is confined to this boundary layer and the radial and axial component of velocity (f and h, respectively) persist outside this layer. The results for the quantities $\varepsilon g_z(0,t)$, $f_z(0,t)$ and $h(\infty,t)/\varepsilon$ are displayed in Figures 5.4.3(a-d). Comparing these figures we see that the fluctuations in $h(\infty,t)$ decrease as $\varepsilon \to 0$. This means that outside the boundary layer the fluid motion becomes stationary (i.e. the outer flow does not depend on t). These numerical results are in agreement with the analytical solutions of ROSENBLAT [5].

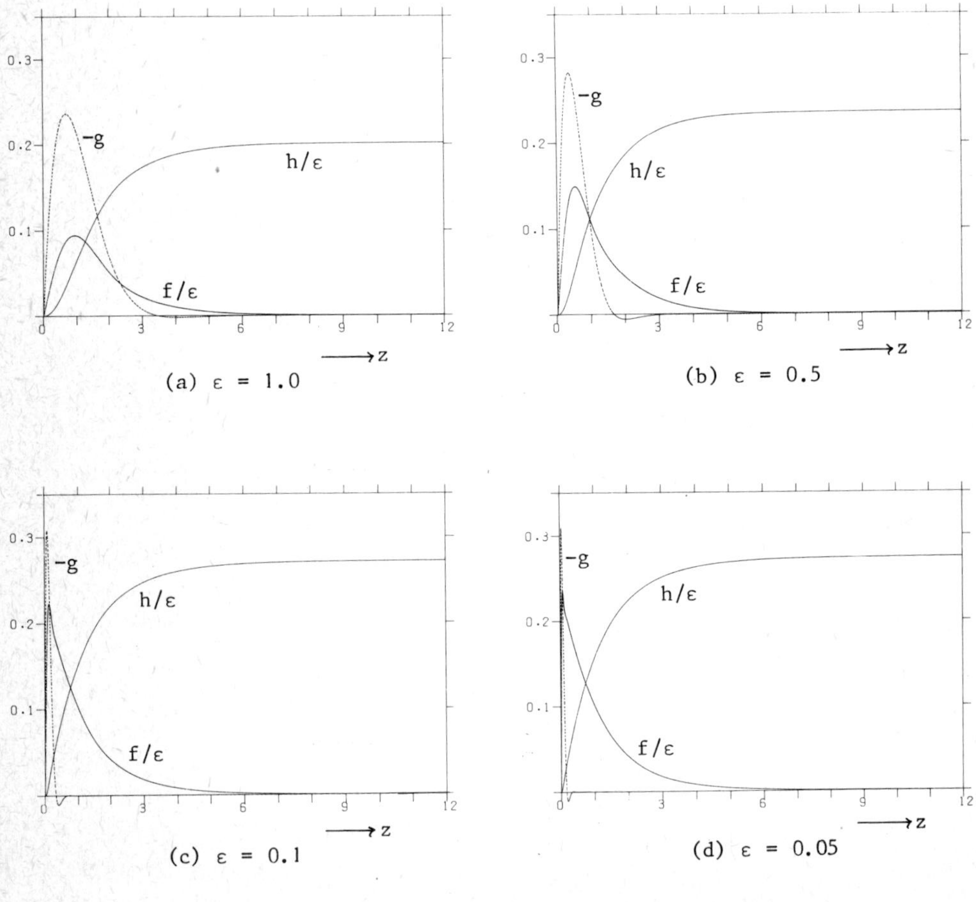

Figure 5.4.2. Velocity profiles.

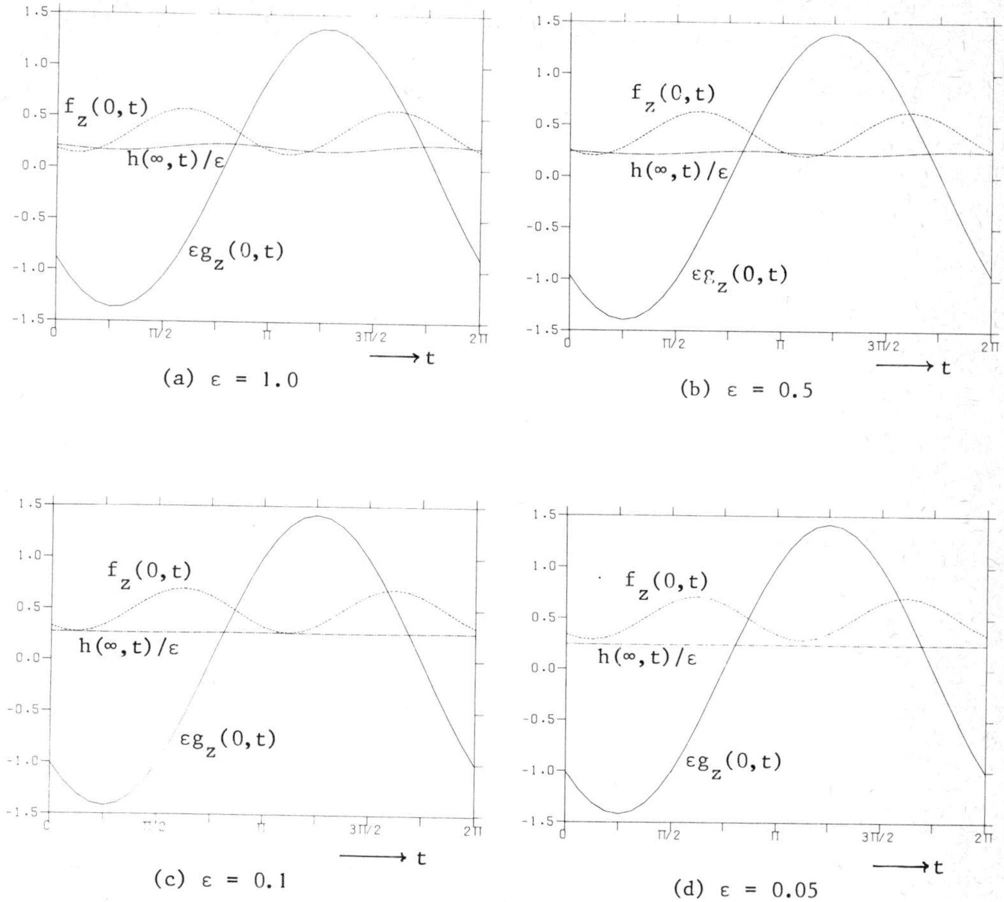

Figure 5.4.3. Axial inflow and shear stresses.

In this chapter we discussed two computational schemes for the calculation of oscillating disk flow in an *infinite* medium. These schemes can also be applied to the rotating flow due to a disk oscillating in a *finite* medium, i.e. at $z = \ell$ there is a second infinite disk. For this two-disk problem numerical results of method A have been reported in [2]. In this paper we encountered the problem that also the low-frequency case sometimes converged slowly. Considering the numerical results of Table 5.1, we also recommend the use of multiple grid methods to compute this type of flow.

Finally, from the results just presented we conclude that for the computation of periodic solutions of the single disk problem for $\varepsilon \leq 1$ the multiple grid method is preferable, whereas for $\varepsilon > 1$ simulation of the physical process may be employed.

REFERENCES TO CHAPTER 5

[1] BENNEY, D.J., *The flow induced by a disk oscillating in its own plane*, Journ. of Fluid Mechanics 18 (1964), pp.385-391.

[2] DIJKSTRA, D., SCHIPPERS, H. & P.J. ZANDBERGEN, *On certain solutions of the non-stationary equations for rotating flow*, Procs 6th International Conference on numerical methods in Fluid Dynamics (Tbilisi, 1978), Springer Verlag, Berlin.

[3] HACKBUSCH, W., *Fast numerical solution of time-periodic parabolic problems by a multigrid method*, SIAM J. Sci. Stat. Comput. 2 (1981), pp.198-206.

[4] RILEY, N., *Oscillating viscous flows*, Mathematika 12 (1965), pp.161-175.

[5] ROSENBLAT, S., *Torsional oscillations of a plane in a viscous fluid*, Journ. of Fluid Mechanics 5 (1959), pp.206-220.

[6] ZANDBERGEN, P.J. & D. DIJKSTRA, *Non-unique solutions of the Navier-Stokes equations for the Kármán switching flow*, Journ. of Engineering Mathematics 11 (1977), pp.167-188.

SUMMARY

Multiple grid methods are studied for solving algebraic systems of equations that occur in numerical methods for Fredholm integral equations of the second kind. In general, the algebraic systems are non-sparse and in practice the dimensions are large, so that iterative schemes are needed. In Chapter 2 various iterative schemes (a.o. four multiple grid methods) are analysed.

Multiple grid methods are iterative schemes that work with a sequence of computational grids of increasing refinement. The solutions of different but related problems on these grids interact with each other to obtain an approximation to the continuous solution of the integral equation. On each grid in a multiple grid process a system of equations is approximately solved by some relaxation scheme (for example: Jacobi relaxation) reducing the oscillating error vectors with short wavelength, compared with the scale of the grid. The components with long wavelength are reduced by a coarse grid correction. Such multiple grid iterative methods have recently received increased attention for solving partial differential equations of elliptic type. In this thesis it is shown that they can also be used advantageously for Fredholm integral equations of the second kind. Theoretical and numerical investigations show that the rates of convergence of the presented multiple grid methods increase as $N \to \infty$, with N the dimension of the finest grid. The multiple grid algorithm that appears to be the most robust one is described in Chapter 3, where it is implemented in an automatic program. This program has been written in the algorithmic language ALGOL 68.

The fast convergence of multiple grid methods for integral equations is established for the following problems from fluid mechanics: (1) calculation of potential flow around aerofoils and (2) calculation of oscillating disk flow. Problem (1) is reformulated as a boundary integral equation of the second kind that is approximated by a first order panel method resulting in a full system of equations. This method is in widespread use for aerodynamic computations. Problem (2) is described by the Navier-Stokes equations. By means of the von Kármán similarity transformations these equations are reduced to a nonlinear system of parabolic equations which are approximated by implicit finite difference techniques. From the periodic conditions in time one obtains a nonlinear operator equation of the second kind.

AUTHOR INDEX

Numbers indicate the pages of the text on which the author's work is referred to.

SUBJECT INDEX

Numbers indicate the pages of the text on which the subjects are defined, treated, etc.

TITLES IN THE SERIES MATHEMATICAL CENTRE TRACTS

(An asterisk before the MCT number indicates that the tract is under preparation).

A leaflet containing an order form and abstracts of all publications mentioned below is available at the Mathematisch Centrum, Kruislaan 413, 1098 SJ Amsterdam, The Netherlands. Orders should be sent to the same address.

MCT 1 T. VAN DER WALT, *Fixed and almost fixed points*, 1963. ISBN 90 6196 002 9.

MCT 2 A.R. BLOEMENA, *Sampling from a graph*, 1964. ISBN 90 6196 003 7.

MCT 3 G. DE LEVE, *Generalized Markovian decision processes, part I: Model and method*, 1964. ISBN 90 6196 004 5.

MCT 4 G. DE LEVE, *Generalized Markovian decision processes, part II: Probabilistic background*, 1964. ISBN 90 6196 005 3.

MCT 5 G. DE LEVE, H.C. TIJMS & P.J. WEEDA, *Generalized Markovian decision processes, Applications*, 1970. ISBN 90 6196 051 7.

MCT 6 M.A. MAURICE, *Compact ordered spaces*, 1964. ISBN 90 6196 006 1.

MCT 7 W.R. VAN ZWET, *Convex transformations of random variables*, 1964. ISBN 90 6196 007 X.

MCT 8 J.A. ZONNEVELD, *Automatic numerical integration*, 1964. ISBN 90 6196 008 8.

MCT 9 P.C. BAAYEN, *Universal morphisms*, 1964. ISBN 90 6196 009 6.

MCT 10 E.M. DE JAGER, *Applications of distrubutions in mathematical physics*, 1964. ISBN 90 6196 010 X.

MCT 11 A.B. PAALMAN-DE MIRANDA, *Topological semigroups*, 1964. ISBN 90 6196 011 8.

MCT 12 J.A.Th.M. VAN BERCKEL, H. BRANDT CORSTIUS, R.J. MOKKEN & A. VAN WIJNGAARDEN, *Formal properties of newspaper Dutch*, 1965. ISBN 90 6196 013 4.

MCT 13 H.A. LAUWERIER, *Asymptotic expansions*, 1966, out of print; replaced by MCT 54.

MCT 14 H.A. LAUWERIER, *Calculus of variations in mathematical physics*, 1966. ISBN 90 6196 020 7.

MCT 15 R. DOORNBOS, *Slippage tests*, 1966. ISBN 90 6196 021 5.

MCT 16 J.W. DE BAKKER, *Formal definition of programming languages with an application to the definition of ALGOL 60*, 1967. ISBN 90 6196 022 3.

MCT 17 R.P. VAN DE RIET, *Formula manipulation in ALGOL 60, part 1*, 1968.
ISBN 90 6196 025 8.

MCT 18 R.P. VAN DE RIET, *Formula manipulation in ALGOL 60, part 2*, 1968.
ISBN 90 6196 038 X.

MCT 19 J. VAN DER SLOT, *Some properties related to compactness*, 1968.
ISBN 90 6196 026 6.

MCT 20 P.J. VAN DER HOUWEN, *Finite difference methods for solving partial differential equations*, 1968. ISBN 90 6196 027 4.

MCT 21 E. WATTEL, *The compactness operator in set theory and topology*, 1968.
ISBN 90 6196 028 2.

MCT 22 T.J. DEKKER, *ALGOL 60 procedures in numerical algebra, part 1*, 1968.
ISBN 90 6196 029 0.

MCT 23 T.J. DEKKER & W. HOFFMANN, *ALGOL 60 procedures in numerical algebra, part 2*, 1968. ISBN 90 6196 030 4.

MCT 24 J.W. DE BAKKER, *Recursive procedures*, 1971. ISBN 90 6196 060 6.

MCT 25 E.R. PAËRL, *Representations of the Lorentz group and projective geometry*, 1969. ISBN 90 6196 039 8.

MCT 26 EUROPEAN MEETING 1968, *Selected statistical papers, part I*, 1968.
ISBN 90 6196 031 2.

MCT 27 EUROPEAN MEETING 1968, *Selected statistical papers, part II*, 1969.
ISBN 90 6196 040 1.

MCT 28 J. OOSTERHOFF, *Combination of one-sided statistical tests*, 1969.
ISBN 90 6196 041 X.

MCT 29 J. VERHOEFF, *Error detecting decimal codes*, 1969. ISBN 90 6196 042 8.

MCT 30 H. BRANDT CORSTIUS, *Exercises in computational linguistics*, 1970.
ISBN 90 6196 052 5.

MCT 31 W. MOLENAAR, *Approximations to the Poisson, binomial and hypergeometric distribution functions*, 1970. ISBN 90 6196 053 3.

MCT 32 L. DE HAAN, *On regular variation and its application to the weak convergence of sample extremes*, 1970. ISBN 90 6196 054 1.

MCT 33 F.W. STEUTEL, *Preservation of infinite divisibility under mixing and related topics*, 1970. ISBN 90 6196 061 4.

MCT 34 I. JUHÁSZ, A. VERBEEK & N.S. KROONENBERG, *Cardinal functions in topology*, 1971. ISBN 90 6196 062 2.

MCT 35 M.H. VAN EMDEN, *An analysis of complexity*, 1971. ISBN 90 6196 063 0.

MCT 36 J. GRASMAN, *On the birth of boundary layers*, 1971. ISBN 90 6196 064 9.

MCT 37 J.W. DE BAKKER, G.A. BLAAUW, A.J.W. DUIJVESTIJN, E.W. DIJKSTRA, P.J. VAN DER HOUWEN, G.A.M. KAMSTEEG-KEMPER, F.E.J. KRUSEMAN ARETZ, W.L. VAN DER POEL, J.P. SCHAAP-KRUSEMAN, M.V. WILKES & G. ZOUTENDIJK, *MC-25 Informatica Symposium* 1971.
ISBN 90 6196 065 7.

MCT 38 W.A. VERLOREN VAN THEMAAT, *Automatic analysis of Dutch compound words*, 1971. ISBN 90 6196 073 8.

MCT 39 H. BAVINCK, *Jacobi series and approximation*, 1972. ISBN 90 6196 074 6.

MCT 40 H.C. TIJMS, *Analysis of (s,S) inventory models*, 1972. ISBN 90 6196 075 4.

MCT 41 A. VERBEEK, *Superextensions of topological spaces*, 1972. ISBN 90 6196 076 2.

MCT 42 W. VERVAAT, *Success epochs in Bernoulli trials (with applications in number theory)*, 1972. ISBN 90 6196 077 0.

MCT 43 F.H. RUYMGAART, *Asymptotic theory of rank tests for independence*, 1973. ISBN 90 6196 081 9.

MCT 44 H. BART, *Meromorphic operator valued functions*, 1973. ISBN 90 6196 082 7.

MCT 45 A.A. BALKEMA, *Monotone transformations and limit laws* 1973. ISBN 90 6196 083 5.

MCT 46 R.P. VAN DE RIET, *ABC ALGOL, A portable language for formula manipulation systems, part 1: The language*, 1973. ISBN 90 6196 084 3.

MCT 47 R.P. VAN DE RIET, *ABC ALGOL, A portable language for formula manipulation systems, part 2: The compiler*, 1973. ISBN 90 6196 085 1.

MCT 48 F.E.J. KRUSEMAN ARETZ, P.J.W. TEN HAGEN & H.L. OUDSHOORN, *An ALGOL 60 compiler in ALGOL 60, Text of the MC-compiler for the EL-X8*, 1973. ISBN 90 6196 086 X.

MCT 49 H. KOK, *Connected orderable spaces*, 1974. ISBN 90 6196 088 6.

MCT 50 A. VAN WIJNGAARDEN, B.J. MAILLOUX, J.E.L. PECK, C.H.A. KOSTER, M. SINTZOFF, C.H. LINDSEY, L.G.L.T. MEERTENS & R.G. FISKER (eds), *Revised report on the algorithmic language ALGOL 68*, 1976. ISBN 90 6196 089 4.

MCT 51 A. HORDIJK, *Dynamic programming and Markov potential theory*, 1974. ISBN 90 6196 095 9.

MCT 52 P.C. BAAYEN (ed.), *Topological structures*, 1974. ISBN 90 6196 096 7.

MCT 53 M.J. FABER, *Metrizability in generalized ordered spaces*, 1974. ISBN 90 6196 097 5.

MCT 54 H.A. LAUWERIER, *Asymptotic analysis, part 1*, 1974. ISBN 90 6196 098 3.

MCT 55 M. HALL JR. & J.H. VAN LINT (eds), *Combinatorics, part 1: Theory of designs, finite geometry and coding theory*, 1974. ISBN 90 6196 099 1.

MCT 56 M. HALL JR. & J.H. VAN LINT (eds), *Combinatorics, part 2: Graph theory, foundations, partitions and combinatorial geometry*, 1974. ISBN 90 6196 100 9.

MCT 57 M. HALL JR. & J.H. VAN LINT (eds), *Combinatorics, part 3: Combinatorial group theory*, 1974. ISBN 90 6196 101 7.

MCT 58 W. ALBERS, *Asymptotic expansions and the deficiency concept in statistics*, 1975. ISBN 90 6196 102 5.

MCT 59 J.L. MIJNHEER, *Sample path properties of stable processes*, 1975. ISBN 90 6196 107 6.

MCT 60 F. GÖBEL, *Queueing models involving buffers*, 1975. ISBN 90 6196 108 4.

*MCT 61 P. VAN EMDE BOAS, *Abstract resource-bound classes, part 1*, ISBN 90 6196 109 2.

*MCT 62 P. VAN EMDE BOAS, *Abstract resource-bound classes, part 2*, ISBN 90 6196 110 6.

MCT 63 J.W. DE BAKKER (ed.), *Foundations of computer science*, 1975. ISBN 90 6196 111 4.

MCT 64 W.J. DE SCHIPPER, *Symmetric closed categories*, 1975. ISBN 90 6196 112 2.

MCT 65 J. DE VRIES, *Topological transformation groups 1 A categorical approach*, 1975. ISBN 90 6196 113 0.

MCT 66 H.G.J. PIJLS, *Locally convex algebras in spectral theory and eigenfunction expansions*, 1976. ISBN 90 6196 114 9.

*MCT 67 H.A. LAUWERIER, *Asymptotic analysis, part 2*, ISBN 90 6196 119 X.

MCT 68 P.P.N. DE GROEN, *Singularly perturbed differential operators of second order*, 1976. ISBN 90 6196 120 3.

MCT 69 J.K. LENSTRA, *Sequencing by enumerative methods*, 1977. ISBN 90 6196 125 4.

MCT 70 W.P. DE ROEVER JR., *Recursive program schemes: Semantics and proof theory*, 1976. ISBN 90 6196 127 0.

MCT 71 J.A.E.E. VAN NUNEN, *Contracting Markov decision processes*, 1976. ISBN 90 6196 129 7.

MCT 72 J.K.M. JANSEN, *Simple periodic and nonperiodic Lamé functions and their applications in the theory of conical waveguides*, 1977. ISBN 90 6196 130 0.

MCT 73 D.M.R. LEIVANT, *Absoluteness of intuitionistic logic*, 1979. ISBN 90 6196 122 X.

MCT 74 H.J.J. TE RIELE, *A theoretical and computational study of generalized aliquot sequences*, 1976. ISBN 90 6196 131 9.

MCT 75 A.E. BROUWER, *Treelike spaces and related connected topological spaces*, 1977. ISBN 90 6196 132 7.

MCT 76 M. REM, *Associations and the closure statement*, 1976. ISBN 90 6196 135 1.

MCT 77 W.C.M. KALLENBERG, *Asymptotic optimality of likelihood ratio tests in exponential families*, 1977. ISBN 90 6196 134 3.

MCT 78 E. DE JONGE & A.C.M. VAN ROOIJ, *Introduction to Riesz spaces*, 1977. ISBN 90 6196 133 5.

MCT 79 M.C.A. VAN ZUIJLEN, *Empirical distributions and rank statistics*, 1977. ISBN 90 6196 145 9.

MCT 80 P.W. HEMKER, *A numerical study of stiff two-point boundary problems*, 1977. ISBN 90 6196 146 7.

MCT 81 K.R. APT & J.W. DE BAKKER (eds), *Foundations of computer science II*, part 1, 1976. ISBN 90 6196 140 8.

MCT 82 K.R. APT & J.W. DE BAKKER (eds), *Foundations of computer science II*, part 2, 1976. ISBN 90 6196 141 6.

MCT 83 L.S. BENTHEM JUTTING, *Checking Landau's "Grundlagen" in the AUTOMATH system*, 1979. ISBN 90 6196 147 5.

MCT 84 H.L.L. BUSARD, *The translation of the elements of Euclid from the Arabic into Latin by Hermann of Carinthia (?) books vii-xii*, 1977. ISBN 90 6196 148 3.

MCT 85 J. VAN MILL, *Supercompactness and Wallman spaces*, 1977. ISBN 90 6196 151 3.

MCT 86 S.G. VAN DER MEULEN & M. VELDHORST, *Torrix I, A programming system for operations on vectors and matrices over arbitrary fields and of variable size*. 1978. ISBN 90 6196 152 1.

*MCT 87 S.G. VAN DER MEULEN & M. VELDHORST, *Torrix II*, ISBN 90 6196 153 X.

MCT 88 A. SCHRIJVER, *Matroids and linking systems*, 1977. ISBN 90 6196 154 8.

MCT 89 J.W. DE ROEVER, *Complex Fourier transformation and analytic functionals with unbounded carriers*, 1978. ISBN 90 6196 155 6.

MCT 90 L.P.J. GROENEWEGEN, *Characterization of optimal strategies in dynamic games*, 1981 . ISBN 90 6196 156 4.

MCT 91 J.M. GEYSEL, *Transcendence in fields of positive characteristic*, 1979. ISBN 90 6196 157 2.

MCT 92 P.J. WEEDA, *Finite generalized Markov programming*, 1979. ISBN 90 6196 158 0.

MCT 93 H.C. TIJMS & J. WESSELS (eds), *Markov decision theory*, 1977. ISBN 90 6196 160 2.

MCT 94 A. BIJLSMA, *Simultaneous approximations in transcendental number theory*, 1978. ISBN 90 6196 162 9.

MCT 95 K.M. VAN HEE, *Bayesian control of Markov chains*, 1978. ISBN 90 6196 163 7.

MCT 96 P.M.B. VITÁNYI, *Lindenmayer systems: Structure, languages, and growth functions*, 1980. ISBN 90 6196 164 5.

*MCT 97 A. FEDERGRUEN, *Markovian control problems; functional equations and algorithms*, . ISBN 90 6196 165 3.

MCT 98 R. GEEL, *Singular perturbations of hyperbolic type*, 1978. ISBN 90 6196 166 1.

MCT 99 J.K. LENSTRA, A.H.G. RINNOOY KAN & P. VAN EMDE BOAS, *Interfaces between computer science and operations research*, 1978. ISBN 90 6196 170 X.

MCT 100 P.C. BAAYEN, D. VAN DULST & J. OOSTERHOFF (eds), *Proceedings bicentennial congress of the Wiskundig Genootschap, part 1*, 1979. ISBN 90 6196 168 8.

MCT 101 P.C. BAAYEN, D. VAN DULST & J. OOSTERHOFF (eds), *Proceedings bicentennial congress of the Wiskundig Genootschap, part 2*, 1979. ISBN 90 6196 169 6.

MCT 102 D. VAN DULST, *Reflexive and superreflexive Banach spaces*, 1978. ISBN 90 6196 171 8.

MCT 103 K. VAN HARN, *Classifying infinitely divisible distributions by functional equations*, 1978. ISBN 90 6196 172 6.

MCT 104 J.M. VAN WOUWE, *Go-spaces and generalizations of metrizability*, 1979. ISBN 90 6196 173 4.

MCT 105 R. HELMERS, *Edgeworth expansions for linear combinations of order statistics*, 1982. ISBN 90 6196 174 2.

MCT 106 A. SCHRIJVER (ed.), *Packing and covering in combinatorics*, 1979. ISBN 90 6196 180 7.

MCT 107 C. DEN HEIJER, *The numerical solution of nonlinear operator equations by imbedding methods*, 1979. ISBN 90 6196 175 0.

MCT 108 J.W. DE BAKKER & J. VAN LEEUWEN (eds), *Foundations of computer science III*, part *1*, 1979. ISBN 90 6196 176 9.

MCT 109 J.W. DE BAKKER & J. VAN LEEUWEN (eds), *Foundations of computer science III*, part *2*, 1979. ISBN 90 6196 177 7.

MCT 110 J.C. VAN VLIET, *ALGOL 68 transput*, part *I*: *Historical review and discussion of the implementation model*, 1979. ISBN 90 6196 178 5.

MCT 111 J.C. VAN VLIET, *ALGOL 68 transput*, part *II*: *An implementation model*, 1979. ISBN 90 6196 179 3.

MCT 112 H.C.P. BERBEE, *Random walks with stationary increments and renewal theory*, 1979. ISBN 90 6196 182 3.

MCT 113 T.A.B. SNIJDERS, *Asymptotic optimality theory for testing problems with restricted alternatives*, 1979. ISBN 90 6196 183 1.

MCT 114 A.J.E.M. JANSSEN, *Application of the Wigner distribution to harmonic analysis of generalized stochastic processes*, 1979. ISBN 90 6196 184 X.

MCT 115 P.C. BAAYEN & J. VAN MILL (eds), *Topological Structures II*, part *1*, 1979. ISBN 90 6196 185 5.

MCT 116 P.C. BAAYEN & J. VAN MILL (eds), *Topological Structures II*, part *2*, 1979. ISBN 90 6196 186 6.

MCT 117 P.J.M. KALLENBERG, *Branching processes with continuous state space*, 1979. ISBN 90 6196 188 2.

MCT 118 P. GROENEBOOM, *Large deviations and asymptotic efficiencies*, 1980. ISBN 90 6196 190 4.

MCT 119 F.J. PETERS, *Sparse matrices and substructures, with a novel implementation of finite element algorithms*, 1980. ISBN 90 6196 192 0.

MCT 120 W.P.M. DE RUYTER, *On the asymptotic analysis of large-scale ocean circulation*, 1980. ISBN 90 6196 192 9.

MCT 121 W.H. HAEMERS, *Eigenvalue techniques in design and graph theory*, 1980. ISBN 90 6196 194 7.

MCT 122 J.C.P. BUS, *Numerical solution of systems of nonlinear equations*, 1980. ISBN 90 6196 195 5.

MCT 123 I. YUHÁSZ, *Cardinal functions in topology - ten years later*, 1980. ISBN 90 6196 196 3.

MCT 124 R.D. GILL, *Censoring and stochastic integrals*, 1980. ISBN 90 6196 197 1.

MCT 125 R. EISING, *2-D systems, an algebraic approach*, 1980. ISBN 90 6196 198 X.

MCT 126 G. VAN DER HOEK, *Reduction methods in nonlinear programming*, 1980. ISBN 90 6196 199 8.

MCT 127 J.W. KLOP, *Combinatory reduction systems*, 1980. ISBN 90 6196 200 5.

MCT 128 A.J.J. TALMAN, *Variable dimension fixed point algorithms and triangulations*, 1980. ISBN 90 6196 201 3.

MCT 129 G. VAN DER LAAN, *Simplicial fixed point algorithms*, 1980. ISBN 90 6196 202 1.

MCT 130 P.J.W. TEN HAGEN et al., *ILP Intermediate language for pictures*, 1980. ISBN 90 6196 204 8.

MCT 131 R.J.R. BACK, *Correctness preserving program refinements: Proof theory and applications*, 1980. ISBN 90 6196 207 2.

MCT 132 H.M. MULDER, *The interval function of a graph*, 1980. ISBN 90 6196 208 0.

MCT 133 C.A.J. KLAASSEN, *Statistical performance of location estimators*, 1981. ISBN 90 6196 209 9.

MCT 134 J.C. VAN VLIET & H. WUPPER (eds), *Proceedings international conference on ALGOL 68*, 1981. ISBN 90 6196 210 2.

MCT 135 J.A.G. GROENENDIJK, T.M.V. JANSSEN & M.J.B. STOKHOF (eds), *Formal methods in the study of language*, part *I*, 1981. ISBN 90 6196 211 0.

MCT 136 J.A.G. GROENENDIJK, T.M.V. JANSSEN & M.J.B. STOKHOF (eds), *Formal methods in the study of language*, part *II*, 1981. ISBN 90 6196 213 7.

MCT 137 J. TELGEN, *Redundancy and linear programs*, 1981. ISBN 90 6196 215 3.

MCT 138 H.A. LAUWERIER, *Mathematical models of epidemics*, 1981. ISBN 90 6196 216 1.

MCT 139 J. VAN DER WAL, *Stochastic dynamic programming, successive approximations and nearly optimal strategies for Markov decision processes and Markov games*, 1980. ISBN 90 6196 218 8.

MCT 140 J.H. VAN GELDROP, *A mathematical theory of pure exchange economies without the no-critical-point hypothesis*, 1981.
ISBN 90 6196 219 6.

MCT 141 G.E. WELTERS, *Abel-Jacobi isogenies for certain types of Fano three-folds*, 1981.
ISBN 90 6196 227 7.

MCT 142 H.R. BENNETT & D.J. LUTZER (eds), *Topology and order structures*, part 1, 1981.
ISBN 90 6196 228 5.

MCT 143 H. J.M. SCHUMACHER, *Dynamic feedback in finite- and infinite dimensional linear systems*, 1981.
ISBN 90 6196 229 3.

MCT 144 P. EIJGENRAAM, *The solution of initial value problems using interval arithmetic. Formulation and analysis of an algorithm*, 1981.
ISBN 90 6196 230 7.

MCT 145 A.J. BRENTJES, *Multi-dimensional continued fraction algorithms*, 1981. ISBN 90 6196 231 5.

MCT 146 C. VAN DER MEE, *Semigroup and factorization methods in transport theory*, 1982. ISBN 90 6196 233 1.

MCT 147 H.H. TIGELAAR, *Identification and informative sample size*, 1982.
ISBN 90 6196 235 8.

MCT 148 L.C.M. KALLENBERG, *Linear programming and finite Markovian control problems*, 1983. ISBN 90 6196 236 6.

MCT 149 C.B. HUIJSMANS, M.A. KAASHOEK, W.A.J. LUXEMBURG & W.K. VIETSCH, (eds), *From A to Z, proceeding of a symposium in honour of A.C. Zaanen*, 1982. ISBN 90 6196 241 2.

MCT 150 M. VELDHORST, *An analysis of sparse matrix storage schemes*, 1982.
ISBN 90 6196 242 0.

MCT 151 R.J.M.M. DOES, *Higher order asymptotics for simple linear Rank statistics*, 1982. ISBN 90 6196 243 9.

MCT 152 G.F. VAN DER HOEVEN, *Projections of Lawless sequences*, 1982.
ISBN 90 6196 244 7.

MCT 153 J.P.C. BLANC, *Application of the theory of boundary value problems in the analysis of a queueing model with paired services*, 1982.
ISBN 90 6196 247 1.

MCT 154 H.W. LENSTRA, JR. & R. TIJDEMAN (eds), *Computational methods in number theory, part I*, 1982.
ISBN 90 6196 248 X.

MCT 155 H.W. LENSTRA, JR. & R. TIJDEMAN (eds), *Computational methods in number theory, part II*, 1982.
ISBN 90 6196 249 8.

MCT 156 P.M.G. APERS, *Query processing and data allocation in distributed database systems*, 1983.
ISBN 90 6196 251 X.

MCT 157 H.A.W.M. KNEPPERS, *The covariant classification of two-dimensional smooth commutative formal groups over an algebraically closed field of positive characteristic*, 1983.
ISBN 90 6196 252 8.

MCT 158 J.W. DE BAKKER & J. VAN LEEUWEN (eds), *Foundations of computer science IV, Distributed systems*, part 1, 1983.
ISBN 90 6196 254 4.

MCT 159 J.W. DE BAKKER & J. VAN LEEUWEN (eds), *Foundations of computer science IV, Distributed systems*, part 2, 1983.
ISBN 90 6196 255 0.

MCT 160 A. REZUS, *Abstract automat*, 1983.
ISBN 90 6196 256 0.

MCT 161 G.F. HELMINCK, *Eisenstein series on the metaplectic group, An algebraic approach*, 1983.
ISBN 90 6196 257 9.

MCT 162 J.J. DIK, *Tests for preference*, 1983.
ISBN 90 6196 259 5

MCT 163 H. SCHIPPERS, *Multiple grid methods for equations of the second kind with applications in fluid mechanics*, 1983.
ISBN 90 6196 260 9.

MCT 164 F.A. VAN DER DUYN SCHOUTEN, *Markov decision processes with continuous time parameter*, 1983.
ISBN 90 6196 261 7.

MCT 165 P.C.T. VAN DER HOEVEN, *On point processes*, 1983.
ISBN 90 6196 262 5.

An asterisk before the number means "to appear"